REVISE EDEXCEL
FUNCTIONAL SKILLS LEVEL 2

English

REVISION WORKBOOK

Series Consultant: Harry Smith

Author: Julie Hughes

To revise all the topics covered in this book, check out:

Revise Functional Skills Level 2
English Revision Guide   9781 292 145815

THE REVISE SERIES
For the full range of Pearson revision titles, visit:
www.pearsonschools.co.uk/revise

Contents

1-to-1 page match with the Level 2 Revision Guide ISBN 978 1 292 14581 5

A small bit of small print

Edexcel publishes Sample Test Materials on its website. This is the official content and this book should be used in conjunction with it. The questions in this book have been written to help you practise what you have learned in your revision. Remember: the real test questions may not look like this.

Your reading and writing tests

1   How long will your reading test last? Answer the question with **one** cross in the box you think is correct.

     ☐   **A**   13 minutes

     ☐   **B**   2 hours

     ☐   **C**   60 minutes

     ☐   **D**   45 minutes

2   How long should you leave at the end of the test for checking your answers?

....

3   List **three** things you should do before you start to answer a question.

....

....

....

....

GUIDED   4   Complete the table about your writing test below. Write the missing words in the first column, and the number of minutes you should spend on each stage in the second column.

Planning Task 1	5 minutes
Writing and .... Task 1	....
Planning Task 2	....
Writing and .... Task 2	....

5   List **two** things you should do during the planning stage of your writing test.

....

....

....

....

Online tools 1

1 Give **two** reasons why it is important to know how to use the online test **before** you start it.

....

....

....

....

> **GUIDED** **2** There are some useful icons across the top of the test screen. Instructions for the most useful ones are printed below. Match the instructions with the correct icon.

Help

Time   You can click this to find out how much time you have left in your test. The time will appear in the bottom left corner of the screen.

You can click this icon if you want a demonstration of how the online test buttons work.

Quit   These buttons move you from question to question.

Previous **Next**   Be very careful with this button. If you click on it and then select 'Yes', you will not be able to return to the test, even if you haven't finished!

3 Label these **four** buttons on the Settings box with explanations about how they can help you in your test.

switch colours ....

zoom reset ....

colour reset ....

↑ ....

Online tools 2

GUIDED 1 The notepad tool takes you to the notepad screen. State **two** ways the notepad is useful during your test.

You can use the notepad to underline key words in questions.

....

....

2 These buttons will be across the top of the screen during your writing test. You can use them to change the layout and look of your writing. List **three** presentation features that these buttons will help you to use. Draw an arrow to the button you are writing about.

| Arial | ∨ ■ ∨ | 16 ∨ | B | *I* | U | ☰ | ☰ | ☰ | ☰ | ☰ |

....

....

....

3 How will these buttons help you if you are unsure about the answer to a question?

✓
Flag   ....

Review   ....

4 In both tests, you will be reminded when you have 5 minutes left. Which of the following should you do during these 5 minutes? Answer the question with **one** cross in the box you think is correct.

☐ **A** Click the 'Quit' button if you have finished.

☐ **B** Use the time to check your answers.

☐ **C** Click the 'Help' button for more instructions.

☐ **D** Use the time to underline key words in the questions.

Reading texts

1   How many texts will you need to read for your reading test?

    ....

2   List **three** things you should identify when reading the texts.

    ....

    ....

    ....

Read this extract from Text B on page 77, then answer the questions that follow.

> **Cycle your way to health**
>
> Cycling is one the best ways to get more active, and can be enjoyed safely by people of all ages from all walks of life.
>
> Cycling can easily be incorporated into your daily life. You can cycle to school, to work, to the shops, or just ride for fun. Adults should do at least 150 minutes of moderate activity each week. Children and young people should attempt 60 minutes of vigorous activity every day. 30 minutes of cycling, which raises your heart-beat and increases your breathing, counts towards these recommended activity targets.
>
> **Before you start**
>
> 1. For short journeys, any good bike will do. If you buy second-hand, consider taking the bike to a specialist shop for servicing before you ride it.
>
> 2. Buy a helmet. It is estimated that 60% of cycling deaths could be prevented by wearing an approved safety helmet. Look out for the BSI safety kite mark to make sure the helmet you buy has passed all safety testing. If you have children, get them into the habit of wearing a helmet as soon as they start cycling, even when riding with stabilisers.

3   What is the theme or topic of the text? Underline where in the text you have identified this.

    ....

4   What is the writer's point of view? Answer the question with **one** cross in the box next to the most appropriate statement.

    ☐ **A** Cycling is an expensive hobby as you need to buy a helmet.

    ☐ **B** It is easy to take up cycling as a hobby.

    ☐ **C** Second-hand bikes are best.

    ☐ **D** Children should do more exercise.

Skimming for details

> **GUIDED**

1   List **three** useful parts of a text to skim for information.

the first sentence of each paragraph

....

....

2   What should you do before skim reading a text?

....

....

Skim read this extract from Text H on page 83 and answer the questions that follow.

Shopping for less

The cost of living is creeping up again, so it's impossible to cut down any more on household bills. Food is just so expensive now, and cutting corners leads to unhealthy food choices.

Wrong! It's all about careful planning and sensible shopping.

Money experts say it's actually possible to slash your shopping bills by as much as half, without resorting to a diet of unhealthy frozen pizza. A lot of what we buy each week is wasted as either we don't eat it in time, or we decide when we get it home that we don't actually need it. We are also wasting money on 'healthy' supplements that we don't even need.

So what simple steps can we take to stay healthy and significantly reduce our shopping bills?

1.   Take a list to the shops. Plan your meals for the week in advance, shop once and buy only what you need.

---

3   What does the title suggest about the main idea of the text?

....

....

4   What do the first sentences of each paragraph suggest about the writer's point of view?

....

....

5   The text uses a numbered list. What does the first item in this list suggest about the main purpose of the text?

....

....

Underlining

Read this extract from Text C on page 78 and answer the questions that follow.

It isn't just cyclists ignoring red lights that annoys those in cars. Cyclists are seen as breaking many of the rules of the road, such as overtaking on both sides of cars, cutting corners, riding on pavements and riding two abreast on narrow roads. The most annoying habit of cyclists, according to David Evans, of the organisation Safety First, <u>is failing to use hand signals when cycling in traffic</u>.

'Car drivers would be fined, or at least seriously warned, if they failed to use their indicators or lights. So why should those who pay nothing to use the roads be treated differently? It is often cyclists behaving irresponsibly who cause serious accidents, but it is usually the car driver who bears the cost.'

Evans does agree that cycling should be encouraged <u>as it is undoubtedly better for our health than sitting in a car</u>. But cyclists be warned – the health benefits do not make you king of the road. Evans wants a tax introduced on cycling to match the tax paid for cars, and also a compulsory test for cyclists: 'At the very least, <u>cyclists should read the Highway Code</u>, particularly if they are thinking of riding to work in heavy traffic.'

Now read this test-style question. You don't have to answer it. Instead, think about what it is asking you to do, then answer the questions that follow.

> 8 Your friend wants to start cycling to work, but is scared of riding in heavy traffic. Using Texts B and C, advise your friend on how she could prepare to cycle safely in heavy traffic.
>
> **(5 marks)**

GUIDED 1 A student has underlined some of the text extract above. Which **two** of the three underlined sections would help you to answer question 8? Explain your choice.

The third section, as reading the Highway Code will help my friend know the rules for riding in traffic.

....

....

2 Which of the underlined sections would not be helpful? Explain your choice.

....

....

3 Now read Text B on page 77 and underline any information that would help you to answer question 8 above. Annotate each of your underlined sections to explain why they are relevant.

Types of question

Read these test-style questions. You don't have to answer them, just look at what they are asking you to do, then answer the questions that follow.

> **11**   You are preparing a presentation about the popularity of cycling. Which text is the most useful when preparing your talk? Give **one** reason for your choice and **one** example to support your answer.
>
> **(3 marks)**
>
> **12**   You are considering the health benefits of cycling. Identify **one** piece of evidence from **each** of the three texts which shows that there are health benefits to cycling.
>
> **(3 marks)**

1   How many texts should you read carefully for each of these questions?

....

2   Question 11 asks for an example. What does this mean?

....

....

⟩ **GUIDED** ⟩   **3**   List the **two** ways you can present evidence in your answer.

You can use an exact quotation from the text.

....

Now read another test-style question and answer the questions that follow.

> **10**   Use Text A and Text B to answer this question. Explain how these texts have different ideas about cycling. Give examples from both texts to support your answer.
>
> **(5 marks)**

4   List **three** things you should remember when answering this type of question.

....

....

....

5   List **two** things you should do before answering a multiple choice question.

....

....

Reading test skills

Read this test-style question. You don't have to answer it, just look at what it is asking you to do, then answer the questions that follow.

> **11** You are preparing a talk about overseas clothing factories. Which text is the most useful when preparing your talk? Give **one** reason for your choice and one example to support your answer.
>
> **(3 marks)**
>
> Text F

1 What **three** steps should you follow when answering this type of question?

....

....

....

2 A student has attempted to answer question 11. What is wrong with the answer?

....

Now read another test-style question and answer the question that follows.

> **9** Give **one** quotation from Text D and **one** quotation from Text F that suggest giving your unwanted clothes to charity is a good idea.
>
> **(2 marks)**

3 Which **one** of the following would **not** be a good way to approach this type of question? Put a cross in the box beside the answer you think is correct.

☐ **A** Write your answer in full sentences.

☐ **B** Read both texts carefully before answering.

☐ **C** Use exact words from each text as quotations.

☐ **D** Underline words that tell you the focus of the question.

Now read another test-style question and answer the questions that follow.

> **8** Your friend wants to avoid wasting money when shopping in sales. Using Text D and Text F, advise your friend on how to avoid wasting money when shopping in the sales.
>
> **(5 marks)**

4 What might be a problem with this question if you know a lot about fashion?

....

....

Had a go ☐ **Nearly there** ☐ **Nailed it!** ☐

Analysing texts

Read the test-style question below. You don't have to answer it. Instead, think about what it is asking you to do, then answer the questions that follow.

---

5   In Text E, the paragraph beginning 'When something catches their eye' implies that rich people:

☐   **A**   are not sure about what to wear

☐   **B**   cannot shop without a personal stylist

☐   **C**   find clothes shopping easy

☐   **D**   have a difficult time when shopping

(1 mark)

---

1   How much of Text E should you read to answer question 5?

....

....

---

7   Explain **two** ways that the writer of Text C tries to convince the reader that car drivers feel angry about cyclists. Give an example to support each answer.

(4 marks)

---

2   Approximately how long should you spend on question 7? Circle the correct answer.

4 minutes   7 minutes   7 ½ minutes   1 minute

3   Which of the following statements about question 7 is true? Answer the question with **one** cross in the box you think is correct.

☐   **A**   You need to explain the writer's purpose.

☐   **B**   You need to explain why car drivers are angry.

☐   **C**   You need to explain the language used by the writer.

☐   **D**   You need to explain how the writer feels about cyclists.

Putting it into practice

You now know what to expect from the questions in the reading test. Prepare for your test by practising:

- reading different types of text and question
- underlining key information
- answering multiple choice questions
- answering short response questions.

Read the following test-style questions. You don't have to answer them, just think carefully about what they are asking you to do.

---

3   What is the **main** purpose of Text D?

....

....

(1 mark)

---

10   Use Text D and Text F to answer this question. Explain how these texts have different ideas about cheap fashion. Give examples from both texts to support your answer.

(5 marks)

---

1   Read the questions carefully. Underline any key words in the questions that will help you to answer correctly.

2   Skim read Text D on page 79. Underline any information that would help you to answer questions 3 and 10 above. Annotate each of your underlined sections to explain why they are relevant to the questions.

3   Skim read Text F on page 81. Underline any information that would help you to answer question 10 above. Annotate each of your underlined sections to explain why they are different from the points you found in Text D for question 10.

4   Using **one** piece of evidence from Text D and **one** from Text F, explain how these two texts have different ideas about cheap fashion.

> You are only being asked to write **part** of an answer on this page. You will need to write a longer answer for a 5-mark question in your test.

....

....

....

....

....

Identifying the main idea

1   The main idea of a text is sometimes clear from the title. Identify the main idea in each of the titles below and write it in your own words.

   How to look good on a budget   ....

   Cycle your way to health   ....

   Superfoods for family health   ....

GUIDED 2   Sometimes the main idea is not clear from the title. Look at this title and then read the rest of the extract. Complete the sentences below.

> **Fast Fashion**
>
> How often do you shop for clothes? Monthly? Weekly? Some people might be surprised to hear that many young people browse for fashion on a daily basis....
>
> ... high street clothing stores have mastered the art of 'fast fashion'. They can put copies of catwalk creations into their stores quickly, easily and very cheaply. In fact, some stores are able to sell designer look-alikes for less than the price of a takeaway for two.

   The title suggests ....

   The first two paragraphs then show that the **main** idea is ....

   ....

GUIDED 3   Sometimes a title suggests a straightforward idea, but the text is actually more complicated. Read this extract from Text F on page 81 and identify the main idea.

> **How cheap are our cheap clothes?**
>
> Buying cheap clothing is ridiculously easy these days, thanks to fast-fashion labels.
>
> But what is the real cost of the rails of cheap clothes we seem unable to do without? A recent study examines the working practices of the top fast-fashion brands, and shines a light on just how unethical they really are.
>
> The only way to produce enough stock to satisfy our demand for cheap clothing is to manufacture it overseas. While recent horror stories about the use of child labour have stopped many of the worst abuses in overseas factories, there is no doubt that conditions are still way below the standards that would have to be adopted in factories in the UK.

   The title suggests ....

   Reading more of the text shows that the **main** idea is actually about ....

   ....

   ....

11

Texts that instruct

Read this extract from Text B on page 77, then answer the questions that follow.

Cycle your way to health

Cycling is one the best ways to get more active, and can be enjoyed safely by people of all ages from all walks of life.

Cycling can easily be incorporated into your daily life. You can cycle to school, to work, to the shops, or just ride for fun. Adults should do at least 150 minutes of moderate activity each week. Children and young people should attempt 60 minutes of vigorous activity every day. 30 minutes of cycling, which raises your heart-beat and increases your breathing, counts towards these recommended activity targets.

Before you start

1   For short journeys, any good bike will do. If you buy second-hand, consider taking the bike to a specialist shop for servicing before you ride it.

2   Buy a helmet.

> **GUIDED** 1   What does the layout of the text suggest about the purpose?

The text has numbered points. This suggests ....

....

2   Texts that instruct use command verbs and straightforward language. Read the extract carefully and find **two** examples of each.

Command verbs ....

....

Straightforward language ....

....

3   What is the intended audience for the text? Underline information in the text that helps you to identify the audience, then write a sentence explaining your choice.

....

....

....

4   Now write a sentence explaining the main purpose of Text B.

> It is not enough in the test to write 'to instruct'. You must explain what the writer is instructing the reader to do.

....

....

Texts that inform

Read this extract from Text A on page 76, then answer the questions that follow.

Cycling – an Olympic legacy?

Cycling has become remarkably popular over the last four years. According to a new report, sales of bikes have increased by 20% per year since 2012. Many people credit this renewed love of the bicycle to the 'Wiggo effect', named after Bradley Wiggins, one of the cyclists in the incredibly successful British team in the 2012 Olympics.

More people than ever are joining cycling clubs, with participation in competitive events increasing by a whopping 130% over the last four years. The government's cycle to work scheme has also seen a surge in interest, up more than 30% in 2013 alone. All of those taking part pay less tax, as well as saving on petrol.

---

1   Which **two** of the following statements about the layout of informative texts are true? Answer the question with a cross in the **two** boxes you think are correct.

   ☐ **A**   They always use bullet points.

   ☐ **B**   They use paragraphs to separate the ideas into smaller sections.

   ☐ **C**   Paragraphs always contain statistics.

   ☐ **D**   Paragraphs are used to explain ideas in detail.

   ☐ **E**   They always use sub-headings.

GUIDED 2   Texts that inform often use formal language, facts and statistics. Read the extract above carefully and find examples of each of these types of language.

Formal language 'participation in competitive events'

Fact ....

Statistic ....

3   What is the intended audience for the text? Underline information in the text that helps you to identify the audience, then write a sentence explaining your choice.

....

....

....

4   Writers often want the reader to take some form of action. Read the whole of Text A on page 76 and write a sentence explaining what action the writer wants the reader to take.

....

....

....

Texts that persuade

Read this extract from Text F on page 81, then answer the questions that follow.

> **How cheap are our cheap clothes?**
>
> Buying cheap clothing is ridiculously easy these days, thanks to fast-fashion labels.
>
> But what is the real cost of the rails of cheap clothes we seem unable to do without? A recent study examines the working practices of the top fast-fashion brands, and shines a light on just how unethical they really are.
>
> The only way to produce enough stock to satisfy our demand for cheap clothing is to manufacture it overseas. While recent horror stories about the use of child labour have stopped many of the worst abuses in overseas factories, there is no doubt that conditions are still way below the standards that would have to be adopted in factories in the UK.
>
> <u>'In the washing room there are lots of chemicals and the ceiling is not high, so it gets very hot and stuffy,' said one woman, who asked not to be named.</u> As many as 600 workers in the women's factory were crammed into a low-ceilinged, window-less room for over eight hours without a break.

 1 Which **two** of the following are often used to make arguments and persuasive writing more convincing? Circle the correct answers.

    (quotations)   statistics   bullet points   paragraphs   command verbs

GUIDED **2** Find the features you identified in question 1. Draw lines to connect the names of the features to examples in the text.

3 The sentence beginning 'As many as 600 workers...' contains which of the following to make readers feel sympathetic? Answer the question with **one** cross in the box you think is correct.

    ☐ **A** a command verb

    ☐ **B** a rhetorical question

    ☐ **C** descriptive language

    ☐ **D** direct address

    ☐ **E** an exclamation

4 Now read all of Text F. What do you think is the **main** purpose of the text?

....

....

Language techniques 1

Read this extract from Text I on page 84, then answer the questions that follow.

> **Is it possible to eat for £12 a week?**
>
> It's mealtime in a typical family home. <u>Two younger children are eating chicken nuggets and chips, a teenager is eating a pasta ready meal and the adults are tucking into a takeaway curry.</u> The total cost is £35.
>
> According to a leading family-support charity, the average UK family now spends more on ready meals, restaurant dining and takeaways than they spend on food for meal preparation. This is leading to a debt mountain for many families, says Tom Brown, Director of the charity Familycrisis.
>
> However, Brown feels that there is an alternative to this debt crisis: 'With careful planning, it is possible for an adult to eat for as little as £12 a week and still have a healthy, balanced diet.'

GUIDED

1.   Identify and underline these **three** different types of language in the extract above. Draw lines to connect the types of language with the examples in the text.

     <u>informal language</u>   descriptive language   emotive language

2.   Choose **one** of the types of language you identified. Explain how the writer has used it to convince the reader that spending less on food is a good idea.

     ....

     ....

     ....

Now read the final paragraph of Text I below and answer the questions that follow.

> To Tom Brown the answer is simple. 'Take a cookery course. Shop carefully and squeeze every last penny out of your household shop.' So, to cut down on that food bill it might be time to live like your grandmother and learn to love your oven.

3.   Writers can use a formal style or an informal, more personal style. Which style is used in this paragraph? Underline a phrase from the extract as an example of the style you have identified.

     ....

     ....

4.   Which of the following from the paragraph above is an example of a command verb? Answer the question with **one** cross in the box you think is correct.

     ☐   **A**   simple

     ☐   **B**   carefully

     ☐   **C**   bill

     ☐   **D**   squeeze

Language techniques 2

Read this extract from Text C on page 78, then answer the questions that follow.

Cyclist vs Driver: a war coming soon to a city near you

In Toronto, they've painted over the cycle lanes. It's not because the streets are unsafe for cyclists. It's not because <u>cars can no longer find space on roads heaving with over-zealous Olympic hopefuls</u>. It's because the car drivers of Toronto are so strongly anti-bike that aggressive behaviour towards cyclists is common.

It isn't just in Toronto that car drivers <u>have declared war on cyclists</u>. Here in England feelings are beginning to run high against those on two wheels, particularly since the government announced new plans to spend even more money making our major cities more cycle friendly.

So what exactly do car drivers hold against their two-wheeled <u>enemies</u>?

> **GUIDED**

1 Identify and underline these **three** different types of language in the extract above. Draw lines to connect the types of language with the examples in the text.

   rhetorical question   <u>hyperbole</u>   repetition

2 Choose **one** of the types of language you identified. Explain how the writer has used it to show the reader how bad things are for cyclists.

   ....

   ....

   ....

Now read the final paragraph of Text C below and answer the question that follows.

Evans does agree that cycling should be encouraged as it is undoubtedly better for our health than sitting in a car. But cyclists be warned – the health benefits do not make you king of the road. Evans wants a tax introduced on cycling to match the tax paid for cars, and also a compulsory test for cyclists: 'At the very least, cyclists should read the Highway Code, particularly if they are thinking of riding to work in heavy traffic.'

---

3 Which **two** of the following can you find in the final paragraph above? Answer the question with a cross in the **two** boxes you think are correct.

   ☐ **A** a rhetorical question

   ☐ **B** counter-argument

   ☐ **C** direct address

   ☐ **D** title

   ☐ **E** a command verb

> Be specific when identifying language and techniques. It is not enough to answer 'question' or 'verb' when you are referring to rhetorical questions or command verbs.

Fact and opinion

Read these three extracts from Text A on page 76, then answer question 1.

> **A** It seems we'd all be fitter, healthier and richer on two wheels.
>
> **B** sales of bikes have increased by 20% per year since 2012
>
> **C** recent research shows that overall bicycle use across the country has remained static

1 Identify which of the above extracts is:

a fact ....

expert evidence ....

an opinion ....

GUIDED **2** Match the explanation to the feature.

can be direct or reported speech   fact

makes a writer's point of view clear   opinion

often contains statistics   expert evidence

Now read this extract from Text C on page 78 and answer the questions that follow.

> Evans does agree that cycling should be encouraged as it is undoubtedly better for our health than sitting in a car. But cyclists be warned – the health benefits do not make you king of the road. Evans wants a tax introduced on cycling to match the tax paid for cars, and also a compulsory test for cyclists: 'At the very least, cyclists should read the Highway Code, particularly if they are thinking of riding to work in heavy traffic.'

3 The sentence starting 'Evans does agree' contains an example of:

☐ **A** reported speech

☐ **B** direct speech

☐ **C** a rhetorical question

☐ **D** a command verb

4 In the extract above, underline an example of expert evidence presented as direct speech.

Putting it into practice

In this section you have revised understanding and identifying:

- the main ideas in a text
- the main purpose of a text
- language techniques
- fact, opinion and expert evidence.

Read Texts A–C on pages 76–78 and answer the test-style questions below.

---

3   What is the **main** purpose of Text A?

....

....

(1 mark)

---

6   In Text B, the sentence 'Think about signing up for a group bike ride' contains an example of:

☐   **A**   an exclamation

☐   **B**   a command verb

☐   **C**   a rhetorical question

☐   **D**   a statement

(1 mark)

---

7   Explain **two** ways the writer of Text C tries to convince the reader that cyclists are a problem on the roads.

1   ....

....

....

2   ....

....

....

(4 marks)

Implicit meaning 1

Read this extract from Text H on page 83, then answer the question that follows.

> The cost of living is creeping up again, so it is impossible to cut down any more on household bills. Food is just so expensive now and cutting corners leads to unhealthy food choices.
>
> Wrong! It's all about careful planning and sensible shopping.
>
> Money experts say it's actually possible to slash your shopping bills by as much as half, without resorting to a diet of cheap frozen pizza.

GUIDED   **1**   Writers do not always state their meaning in a straightforward way. Explain the implied meaning of the following phrases from the extract above.

'creeping up again' ....

....

'cutting corners' This suggests that food is so expensive that people are no longer

able to shop properly.

'slash your shopping bills' ....

....

Now read this extract from Text E on page 80 and a student's annotations about implied meaning.

> When something catches their eye, they just throw a wad of money at it, without ever
> bothering to look at the price tag. If they're unsure about what suits them, they have
> personal stylists to tell them what looks good and what doesn't. If they don't like something
> when they take it home, they can just leave it in the bag.
>
> —— they can afford to pay people to help them shop
>
> they buy things they don't need and can afford to forget about them
>
> they can buy anything they see
>
> they carry loads of cash around with them

2   Use the student's annotations above to help you answer this test-style question:

> **5**   In Text E, the paragraph beginning 'When something catches their eye' implies that rich people:
>
> ☐   **A**   are not sure about what to wear
>
> ☐   **B**   cannot shop without a personal stylist
>
> ☐   **C**   find clothes shopping easy
>
> ☐   **D**   have a difficult time when shopping
>
>   **(1 mark)**

Implicit meaning 2

Read this extract from Text E on page 80, then answer the questions that follow.

> 2. Buy from charity shops. Don't be afraid to root around and take your time. Dive into those tubs of scarves and bags and hats. When you find something wonderful, congratulate yourself. You'll be helping the environment as well as donating to a good cause, as charity shopping stops piles of clothes being dumped into landfill sites.
>
> 3. Invest in a few timeless classics, such as black trousers and a black jacket. By adding inexpensive accessories, or items you have found in a sale, you can put together several different outfits.
>
> 4. Sell, or swap, clothes that you don't wear any more. It's way more environmentally friendly than just dumping them in the bin. There are several online sites specialising in second-hand clothing and it is easy to take a picture of the clothes on your phone. If you don't want to sell, you could invite friends round for regular swapping parties. One friend's expensive mistake could be your new little black dress.

GUIDED 1   Give **two** quotations from the extract above that suggest that shopping in charity shops could be fun.

When you find something wonderful, congratulate yourself.

....

....

2   Give **one** quotation from the extract above that conveys the view that dressing well does not have to cost a lot of money.

....

....

3   Give **one** quotation from the extract above that conveys the view that people should be more responsible when getting rid of unwanted clothes.

> Be careful, as there may be more than one suitable quotation. Read the question carefully to make sure you give the correct number of quotations from each text.

....

....

....

Point of view

Read the following test-style question and answer the questions that follow.

> **1** The writer of Text A believes that:
>
>   ☐ **A** everybody can benefit from cycling
>
>   ☐ **B** more older people are taking up cycling
>
>   ☐ **C** we should all start cycling to work
>
>   ☐ **D** more people than ever have started cycling
>
> **(1 mark)**

1 How much of Text A do you need to read in order to answer the above question correctly? Circle the correct answer.

the first paragraph   the first sentence of each paragraph   the whole text

2 Use the words below to fill in the blanks in the following instructions about working out the point of view.

| facts   language   biased   opinions |

Look for the writer's ...., which tell you how the writer feels about the topic.

Interesting .... such as 'whopping' can also help you work out the writer's

point of view. Find .... and statistics to help you understand the topic. This

information can also help you work out why the writer feels the way he does. If the writer only

writes about one point of view, then it means the text is ....

3 Use your answers to questions 1 and 2 to find the correct answer to the test-style question 1 above.

Now read Text I on page 84 and answer the questions that follow.

⟩**GUIDED**⟩ **4** Which **two** of the following quotations suggest that the writer feels people spend too much money on food? Answer the question with a cross in the **two** boxes you think are correct.

   ☐ **A** 'The adults are tucking into a takeaway curry.'

   ☒ **B** 'This is leading to a debt mountain for many families'

   ☐ **C** 'No more splashing out on Sunday lunch at your local pub.'

5 Find **one** fact and **one** opinion that suggest the writer believes it is possible to spend less on food.

Fact ....

Opinion ....

Putting it into practice

In this section you have revised implicit meaning, and writers' point of view and bias.

Read Texts D and E on pages 79–80, then answer the following test-style questions.

1　The writer of Text D believes that:

☐　**A**　people buy far too many cheap clothes

☐　**B**　it is not necessary to spend a lot on clothes

☐　**C**　people should buy a new outfit for every special occasion

☐　**D**　we should replace our clothes every season　**(1 mark)**

2　In Text D, what do the following quotations suggest about the writer's view of cheap fashion?

'less than the price of a takeaway for two'

....

....

'you just need to play the game'

....

....

(2 marks)

5　In Text E, the paragraph beginning, 'Sell, or swap, clothes…' implies that:

☐　**A**　buying second-hand clothes is better than buying new

☐　**B**　selling your old clothes is a responsible thing to do

☐　**C**　you should sell all your old clothes online

☐　**D**　buying new clothes is not environmentally friendly　**(1 mark)**

9　Give **one** quotation from Text D and **one** quotation from Text E that suggest giving your unwanted clothes to charity is a good idea.

Quotation from Text D

....

....

Quotation from Text E

....

....

(2 marks)

Had a go ☐   Nearly there ☐   Nailed it! ☐

Using more than one text

> **GUIDED** 1   List **four** steps that will help you when using more than one text.

Look at the marks available. If only 1 mark is available for a quotation, don't waste time by finding more than one quotation.

....

....

....

....

....

Read Texts G and H on pages 82 and 83 and this test-style question, then answer the questions that follow.

> 10   Use Text G and Text H on pages 82 and 83 to answer this question. Explain how these texts present different ideas about healthy eating. Give examples from both texts to support your answer.
>
> **(5 marks)**

2   Which of the following is **not** good advice when answering a question like question 10 above? Answer the question with **one** cross in the box you think is correct.

☐ **A** You will need a balanced answer that covers both texts equally.

☐ **B** You will need to write a longer answer as it is worth 5 marks.

☐ **C** You can use whichever two of the texts you think is most suitable.

☐ **D** You should make it very clear which text you are writing about.

3   Which **one** of the following quotations would **not** be suitable for answering question 10 above?

☐ **A** 'eating cheaply can mean missing out on vital healthy nutrients'

☐ **B** 'an adult can eat for as little as £12 and still have a healthy, balanced diet'

☐ **C** 'Superfoods are available in capsule form from every supermarket these days.'

> Always read the question carefully to find out which texts you should use. Here, one of the quotations comes from a text not specified in the question.

4   Explain why the quotation you have picked is **not** suitable for answering question 10.

....

....

....

Selecting quotations

> **GUIDED**

1 The statements in the table describe quotations and paraphrases. Tick the right word(s) in the table to match each description.

	Description	Quotation	Paraphrase
A	a group of words taken from a text or speech	✓	
B	a statement that keeps the original meaning but is reworded		
C	you can use this if a question asks for an example or evidence paraphrase		
D	it is not necessary to use whole sentences		

Read this test-style question and the extract from Text F on page 81 and answer the questions that follow.

---

7 Explain **two** ways the writer of Text F tries to convince the reader that cheap fashion has led to poor working conditions.

Give an example to support each answer.

(3 marks)

The only way to produce enough stock to satisfy our demand for cheap clothing is to manufacture it overseas. While recent horror stories about the use of child labour have stopped many of the worst abuses in overseas factories, there is no doubt that conditions are still way below the standards that would have to be adopted in factories in the UK.

---

2 Which of the following answers should have used inverted commas (' ')? Put a cross in the box next to the answer you think is correct.

☐ **A** The writer uses emotive language like horror stories and abuse to highlight how cheap clothing has led to poor working conditions in the past.

☐ **B** The writer uses a counter-argument by saying that not many factories still use children as labour.

3 Add inverted commas in the correct places to the answer you identified in question 2.

4 Read the rest of Text F on page 81 and find one other answer to question 7 above. Use either a quotation or a paraphrase in your answer.

> Notice that the quotation example for question 2 above uses only a few words from the text, but they still address the focus of the question. Try not to waste time copying out large chunks of the text.

....

....

....

Using texts 1

Read the test-style question and answer the questions that follow.

> **11** You are preparing a talk about family eating habits.
>
> Which text is the most useful when preparing your talk?
>
> Give **one** reason for your choice and **one** example to support your answer.
>
> **(2 marks)**

1 Both Texts G and I mention family eating. Read these two short extracts and decide which text is the most suitable as an answer to question 11 above. Circle the letter of the text.

> **Text G**
>
> To keep your family healthy, you should plan to use nutritional superfoods on a regular basis. It might cost a bit more, but it's really easy to add nutrient-rich, tasty foods to your weekly menus and create delicious feasts that not only taste amazing, but will also bring long-term health benefits.

> **Text I**
>
> It's mealtime in a typical family home. Two younger children are eating chicken nuggets and chips, a teenager is eating a pasta ready meal and the adults are tucking in to a takeaway curry. The total cost is £35.

2 Why is the text you have chosen the most suitable?

....

....

....

3 Underline an example in the text you chose that you could use in your answer.

> This question asks for an 'example', which means that you can either use a quotation or paraphrase the text.

4 Now read Texts G–I all the way through. Which would be the most helpful if you were preparing a presentation about how to keep a family healthy on a budget? Give **one** reason for your choice and **one** example to support your answer.

Text..

Reason ....

....

Example ....

....

Using texts 2

⟩**GUIDED**⟩ **1** Fill in the blanks in these instructions for answering questions about more than one text. Use the words in the box below.

focus	underline	question	~~paragraph~~	skim

Read the .... carefully and underline the ....

.... read each text in turn to find the best places to look for information.

Stop and read the paragraph you have identified when skim reading.

.... useful parts of the text as you read.

2 When skim reading a text to find evidence or examples, which of the following should you look out for? Answer the question with **one** cross in the box you think is correct.

☐ **A** long paragraphs

☐ **B** quotations in inverted commas

☐ **C** key words from the question

☐ **D** underlined sections

Now read a test-style question about the texts on pages 82–84.

---

12 You are wondering about the health benefits of eating more fruit and vegetables.

Identify **one** piece of evidence from **each** of the three texts which shows that there are health benefits to eating more fruit and vegetables.

(3 marks)

---

3 Follow the steps above to find answers within each of the texts to this test-style question.

Text G ....

....

....

Text H ....

....

....

Text I ....

....

....

Putting it into practice

In this section you have revised:
- using quotations and examples
- using information from more than one text.

Read the texts on pages 76–78 and answer the following test-style questions.

---

11 You are preparing a talk about the popularity of cycling. Which text is the most useful when preparing your talk?

Give **one** reason for your choice and **one** example to support your answer.

Text ....

Reason ....

....

Example ....

(3 marks)

> Always look at how many marks are available for a question. These questions are both worth 3 marks. This means you will need to correctly complete all three parts of each question to get full marks.

---

12 You are thinking of taking up cycling and want to understand the health benefits.

Identify **one** piece of evidence from **each** of the three texts which shows that there are health benefits to taking up cycling.

Text A ....

....

Text B ....

....

Text C ....

....

(3 marks)

Summarising 1

1   Which of the words below does **not** mean 'summarise'? Circle the answer(s) you think is/are correct.

sum up   condense   expand on   give an account of   recap

Read this test-style question and answer the questions that follow.

13   Which statement below is an accurate summary of points made in the texts?

☐   **A**   Texts A and C claim that cycling is becoming more popular.

☐   **B**   Texts B and C argue that cycling is not dangerous.

☐   **C**   Texts A and B promote the idea that cycling is healthy.

☐   **D**   Texts A and B state that cycling is easy to do every day.

(1 mark)

2   Questions like question 13 above will ask you to identify which statement is an accurate summary of the texts. Use the words below to fill the gaps in the following instructions.

| options   evidence   consider   main ideas   wrong |

Read each of the answer .... carefully.

.... each one in turn. By the time you answer this type of question

you should have read all three texts in detail and identified the ....
and points of view.

Reject those that are obviously ....

If you are unsure about an option, go back and try to find ....

3   Use the instructions in question 2 to answer question 13 above.

4   Why is option D **not** the correct answer to question 13?

....

....

> **GUIDED**   5   Read Texts B and C on pages 77 and 78 carefully. Complete this sentence to summarise the main ideas in the texts.

Texts B and C both stress the importance of ....

....

....

Summarising 2

Read this test-style question and answer the questions that follow.

> **10** Use Text H and Text I to answer this question.
>
> Explain how these texts have similar ideas about healthy eating on a budget.
>
> Give examples from both texts to support your answer.
>
> **(3 marks)**

 1 The question above asks for similarities between the texts. Match up the following quotations from Text H on page 83 and Text I on page 84 to make them relevant to question 10 above.

Text H		Text I	
A	'Plan your meals for the week in advance'	**1**	'Take a cookery course.'
B	'Home-made sauces cost at least a third less than sauces in jars.'	**2**	'With careful planning, an adult can eat for as little as £12'
C	'Learn to cook'	**3**	'eating more vegetarian meals using healthy fruit and vegetables'
D	'Go vegetarian for at least one meal a week.'	**4**	'the sauce must be home-made'

GUIDED **2** Now use the quotations to summarise **two** similarities between the texts.

Both texts suggest that to eat healthily on

a budget you should learn to cook. Text H

tells the reader to 'learn to cook' and Text I

suggests taking cookery lessons.

> Notice that this answer makes it clear which text is being referred to. It also uses a quotation for one text and a paraphrase for the other.

....

....

....

....

Writing a longer answer

GUIDED   1   When writing a longer answer you will need to signpost your ideas. List **three** words or phrases you can use to do this.

Firstly,

....

....

2   Give **two** phrases that can be used to introduce an example or quotation.

....

....

GUIDED   3   List six adverbials that can be used to compare and summarise texts.

Similarities	Differences
similarly	however

Read this test-style question and answer the question that follows.

> 10   Use Text D and Text F to answer this question.
>
> Explain how these texts have different ideas about the overseas factories that make cheap clothes.
>
> Give examples from both texts to support your answer.   **(5 marks)**

GUIDED   4   Both texts mention that factories are inspected. Use examples about the inspections to write a paragraph in answer to question 10 above. Signpost your answer by using words and phrases from questions 1–3 on this page.

One difference is what the texts say about factory inspections. For instance, Text D ....

....

....

....

....

> Notice that this answer makes it clear which text is being referred to. Always make this clear and use evidence. As this question asks for an example, you could either use a quotation or paraphrase the text.

Responding to a text 1

1   Here is some advice for answering questions about audience needs. Fill in the blanks using the words below.

select	particular	advise	purpose	relevant

You will need to show that you can .... and use ....

information from texts to suit the needs of a .... audience. Thinking

about the .... of the text will help – look out for information that is intended

to .... the reader to do something.

Read the following test-style question and answer the questions that follow.

> 4   Give **one** reason why Text B is the most suitable for people who want to help their children cycle safely.
>
>   **(1 mark)**

2   Which audience do you need to think about for the question above?

   ....

3   What is the focus of the question?

   ....

4   Which of the following is a correct answer to question 4 above? Answer the question with **one** cross in the box you think is correct.

   ☐ **A**   Text B states that you should wear a helmet.

   ☐ **B**   Text B gives advice about wearing a helmet at all times.

   ☐ **C**   Text B gives advice about cycling.

   ☐ **D**   Text B is a leaflet.

5   Look at question 4 again. Explain why you did not choose the other two options.

   ....

   ....

Responding to a text 2

1   The sentences below tell you how to answer longer questions about audience needs. Which one is **not** good advice? Answer the question with **one** cross in the box you think is correct.

☐ **A**   Read both texts in turn before answering.

☐ **B**   Use signpost words and phrases to structure your answer.

☐ **C**   Write more about the first text.

☐ **D**   Make it clear which text you are writing about.

Read this test-style question and answer the questions that follow.

> **8**   Your friend wants to dress well but does not have much money to spend on clothes.
>
> Using Text D and Text E, advise your friend how to dress well on a budget.
>
> **(5 marks)**

2   The tables show useful evidence from Text D and Text E. Match up the pairs of quotations that make sense together.

Text D
A 'charity store sales are now booming'
B 'value fashion stores need to get rid of unsold stock on a regular basis.'
C 'accessorise these with fast fashion to change your look every season.'

Text E
1 'there is always a sale of some sort on somewhere'
2 'Invest in a few timeless classics'
3 'Buy from charity shops.'

GUIDED 3   A student has written one paragraph of an answer to the test-style question above. Use your answers to question 2 to finish the second paragraph.

Firstly, to dress well on a budget you could shop in the sales. Text D says value

fashion shops sell off their stock on a regular basis and Text E states that there is

always a sale on somewhere.

Secondly, you could ....

....

....

....

> Notice that this answer uses adverbials like 'firstly' and 'secondly' to signpost the answer. These also make it very clear which text is being talked about.

Putting it into practice

In this section you have revised:

- summarising information from more than one text
- using texts to respond to audience needs
- writing longer answers.

> Remember to look at how many marks are available for each question and plan your time accordingly. Don't spend too long on a question that is only worth one mark!

Read the texts on pages 83 and 84 and answer the following test-style questions.

---

4   Give **one** reason why Text H is the most helpful text for single people living alone.

....

....

(1 mark)

---

8   Your friend has a low income and is worried about feeding her family on a budget.

Using Text H and Text I, advise your friend how to feed her family well on a budget.

....

....

....

....

....

....

(5 marks)

---

13   Which statement below is an accurate summary of the points made in the texts? Put a cross in the box you think is correct.

☐   **A**   Texts G and H both stress the need to buy superfoods to stay healthy.

☐   **B**   Texts G and I both give examples of how to cook at home.

☐   **C**   Texts H and I both stress the advantages of cooking at home.

☐   **D**   Texts G and I both suggest that food is becoming more expensive.

(1 mark)

Using a dictionary for reading

1   Use a dictionary to find out the meanings of these words from Texts D and F.

charter ....

....

rummage ....

....

Before using a dictionary, always try to work out the meaning of a word by reading it in context. Read this passage from Text F on page 81, then answer the questions that follow.

> The only way to produce enough stock to satisfy our demand for cheap clothing is to <u>manufacture</u> it overseas. While recent horror stories about the use of child <u>labour</u> have stopped many of the worst abuses in overseas factories, there is no doubt that conditions are still way below the standards that would have to be <u>adopted</u> in factories in the UK. ...
>
> A few top fashion brands actively advertise that they do not use any overseas factories that use '<u>sweatshop</u>' style labour. But they tend to be the top end, designer label brands. However, if we want to help improve working conditions overseas and help the environment, perhaps we might be better off shopping for rich people's <u>cast-offs</u> in charity shops. That way, your money goes to a good cause, not to a company that treats its employees like cattle.

2   Without using a dictionary, work out the meaning of the underlined words and write them below in your own words.

manufacture ....

....

labour...

....

adopted ....

....

sweatshop ....

....

cast-offs...

....

3   Now look up the words in a dictionary and check your answers.

> Be careful – some words have more than one meaning. Read the whole sentence carefully to make sure you understand how it is being used in this text.

Avoiding common mistakes

Look at a student's answers to two test-style questions, then answer the questions that follow.

> **3**   What is the **main** purpose of Text G?
>
>   benefits of superfoods
>
>   **(1 mark)**
>
> **4**   Give **one** reason why Text H is the most useful for a person who has a fridge freezer and wants to use it to save money on food.
>
>   it's got advice about saving money on food
>
>   **(1 mark)**

GUIDED   **1**   What common mistake has been made in the answer to question 3 above?

     The student has not read the question carefully and has given the topic of the text,

     not the ....

2   Which common mistake has been made in the answer to question 4 above?

....

....

3   What could the student have done after reading the question to help find the correct answers?

....

....

Now read another answer to a test-style question and answer the question that follows.

> **7**   Explain **two** ways the writer of Text I tries to convince the reader that it is possible to eat healthily on a budget.
>
>   **1**   'No more splashing out on Sunday lunch'
>
>   **2**   uses statistics
>
>   **(2 marks)**

4   The student has given two incorrect answers. Read the question carefully, then read Text I on page 84 and give **two** correct answers.

....

....

Checking your work

1   How much time should you save at the end of your test to check your answers? Circle your answer.

    1 minute   5 minutes   10 minutes

GUIDED   2   List **three** things that you should do during this time.

    Check you have completed all parts of a question correctly.

    ....

    ....

Now read a student's answers to three test-style questions and answer the questions that follow.

---

9   Give **one** quotation from Text D and **one** quotation from Text E that suggest giving your unwanted clothes to charity is a good idea.

    Text D it stops all our unwanted clothes from being dumped into overcrowded

    landfill sites.

    Text E the money goes to good causes

    (2 marks)

---

5   In Text E, the sentence 'Rich people have it easy, don't they?' is an example of:

    ☐ **A** a statement

    ☒ **B** reported speech

    ☐ **C** a command

    ☒ **D** a rhetorical question

    (2 marks)

---

11   You are preparing a presentation on the success of charity clothing shops.
     Which text would be the most useful when preparing your presentation?
     Give **one** reason for your choice and **one** example to support your answer.

     Text: D

     Reason: there have been knock-on benefits for the charity sector
     Example: 'increases in sales of over 100% in the last year alone'

     (3 marks)

---

3   Read the test-style questions carefully and underline key words.

4   Using your answer to question 2, read the student's answers carefully and correct the mistakes.

Writing test skills

> **GUIDED**   1   Read these explanations of the skills you will need in your writing test. Fill the gaps with the words at the bottom of each section.

Writing in the correct style

This means your .... should be .... but to the *point*.

Your writing must also seem *believable* to your ....

| ~~believable~~   detailed   audience   writing   ~~point~~ |

Writing clearly

This means that .... ideas are clearly .... and made

.... for your audience to ....

| difficult   follow   easy   explained |

Using the right features for different purposes

Different purposes require different writing styles. For instance, writing to ....

needs to use features that will make your audience take .... or .... in a

particular way. Your writing needs to use the right .... to fit your ....

| think   action   persuade   purpose   style |

2   Your writing will need to contain a range of sentence structures and paragraphs. When should you start a new paragraph?

....

....

....

3   You should vary your sentence structures. Why is this important?

....

....

....

Writing test questions

Look at this test-style task. You don't need to answer it. Read it carefully, then answer the questions that follow.

TASK B

INFORMATION

Recently your local council agreed plans to make your town centre a pedestrian-only zone. This has led to serious traffic congestion and parking problems in the streets just outside this area. You decide to write an article for your community newsletter about this issue.

You make the following notes:

- There are not enough car parking spaces on the outskirts of town.
- Cars are being parked dangerously on the pavement.
- Residents cannot now park outside their own houses.
- Shops in the town are suffering as people can't park.
- Emergency vehicles find it difficult to get into the centre of town.
- Shops are unable to take deliveries except in the very early hours.

WRITING TASK

Write an article for your community newsletter.

In your article you may:

- describe the issue caused by the pedestrian-only zone
- explain what the long-term effects might be
- state what you think should be done about the issue.

---

1   Why is the information part of the question useful?

....

2   Why is it a good idea to underline key words in the question?

....

3   Identify the audience, purpose and format for the above task. Explain your answers.

Audience   ....

....

Purpose   ....

....

Format   ....

....

Letters, emails and reports

Look at Task D (page 87) below. You don't need to answer it. Read it carefully, then answer the questions that follow.

> You run a local charity that is in need of funds. You decide to apply for a charity grant on behalf of the charity. Write your letter of application to:
>
> Brian Edwards, Venture Volunteering, 4 Forest Lane, Burstone, BG1 4HH.
>
> **In your letter you should:**
>
> - describe the aims of your charity
> - explain why you need the money
> - describe exactly what difference the money could make to the local community.

1   Which of the following greetings is most suitable for the task? Answer the question with **one** cross in the box you think is correct.

    ☐   **A**   Dear Sir

    ☐   **B**   Dear Mr Edwards

    ☐   **C**   Dear Brian

    ☐   **D**   Dear Sir or Madam

GUIDED   **2**   Letters can use headings to make the topic clear. Which of the following is a suitable heading for this letter? Answer the question with **one** cross in the box you think is correct.

    ☐   **A**   £10,000 can change local lives!

    ☒   **B**   Charity Grant

    ☐   **C**   An Application

    ☐   **D**   Do you want to change local lives?

3   Why is option B the most suitable heading for the task?

    ....

    ....

4   Imagine the task above has asked you to include a report explaining why your charity needs funds. Write a suitable title and a brief introduction giving the main facts about the charity.

    Title   ....

    Introduction   ....

    ....

    ....

    ....

Articles and reviews

Look at this information from Task B on page 86. Read it carefully, then answer the questions that follow.

> You decide to write an article for your community newsletter about this issue. You make the following notes:
>
> - There are not enough car parking spaces on the outskirts of town.
> - Cars are being parked dangerously on the pavement.
> - Residents cannot now park outside their own houses.
> - Shops in the town are suffering as people can't park.
> - Emergency vehicles find it difficult to get into the centre of town.
> - Shops are unable to take deliveries except in the very early hours.

1   Think of **two** suitable headlines for an article about the pedestrian-only zone, using a rhetorical question or a challenging statement.

....

....

2   Articles also use sub-headings to organise ideas. Think of **two** suitable sub-headings for the article, using the information section of the task.

....

....

Now read this information from Task C on page 86 and answer the questions that follow.

> All our trams are brand new, clean and ultra-reliable!
>
> We can promise that:
>
> - 99% of our trams run on time
> - our drivers are always friendly, courteous and helpful
> - our tram stops are clean, safe and well-lit.

3   Think of a suitable title for a review of the new tram route.

....

....

GUIDED 4   Reviews need engaging openings that give the reader more details about the writer's opinion. Finish this opening for a review of the new tram route.

> Articles and reviews can look very similar, so make sure you know the difference.

The carpet of litter wasn't a great start to my first journey ....

....

Speeches

Look at this information from Task E on page 88. Read it carefully, then answer the questions that follow.

> **Sharpness Woods**
>
> Estrick Council announce that a planning application is to be considered with regard to Sharpness Woods and the Sharpness Adventure Playground site. This application will be for the sale of the land for the development of houses and retail premises.
>
> Comments on the application will be heard at a public meeting to be held in August. Those wishing to speak at the meeting should submit their comments in writing to the Council no later than 31 July.

GUIDED

1   If this task had asked for a speech to be delivered at the public meeting, you would need an effective opening. Speeches often start with a rhetorical question. Think of **two** possible openers for your speech about the Adventure Playground.

Don't our children deserve a safe and natural place to play?

....

....

2   Speeches can also start with a bold statement. Think of another opening using a bold or challenging statement.

....

....

3   Facts, statistics and opinions can be used to back up your points and make them sound trustworthy. Think of some facts, statistics and opinions for the speech above.

Fact   ....

....

Statistic   ....

....

Opinion   ....

....

4   Now write a strong, concise ending.

....

....

....

> Speeches often end with a warning or thought-provoking question.

Putting it into practice

You now know what to expect from your writing tasks, what skills they will test and what formats you will have to use.

Read the test-style tasks below from page 85 and page 88. You don't need to complete them. Instead, think about what they are asking you to do.

TASK A

Write an email to David, offering to help in one or more areas.

In your email you should:

- identify any group that interests you and explain why
- describe what qualities or experience you have that make you suitable as a volunteer.

You may include any other information.

TASK E

You walk your dog in the woods and your children use the adventure playground. You decide to write a letter setting out your objections to the planning application. Write to Ms Tracey Bancroft, Head of Planning, Estrick Council, 3 Oak Lane, Estrick, BR2 5NG.

In your letter you should:

- state whether you agree or disagree with Estrick Council's proposals
- give detailed reasons to support your views
- state clearly what action you want Estrick Council to take.

---

1   Underline the key words in the task that will help you to identify the audience, purpose and format.

2   Complete this table with planning notes about what style and features are needed for each task.

	Email task	Letter task
Topic		
Audience		
Purpose		
Format		

Inform, explain, describe, review

Read the test-style task below and the information section on page 91. You don't need to complete it. Instead, think about what it is asking you to do.

> **TASK H**
>
> Write a report for your school/college/workplace on how to spend the technology budget. In your report you should:
>
> • explain what technology your school/college/workplace needs
> • explain the advantages and disadvantages of each of the schemes
> • make your recommendation and give your reasons.

GUIDED

1 Writing that informs and explains needs to be organised to make it easy to follow. A student has written the following notes for the task above. In which order should the ideas be presented in the report? Number them from 1 to 5.

Signage best option | 5 |

Signage – students would be motivated if work was displayed | ☐ |

Visitors' system – saves staff costs on reception | ☐ |

Signage – creates extra work as needs staff to update regularly | ☐ |

Visitors' system – no real advantage to students | ☐ |

2 Informative writing needs headings and sub-headings. Think of **two** sub-headings for the report ideas above.

....

....

3 Which **two** of the following statements about writing to describe are true? Answer the question with a cross in the **two** boxes you think are correct.

☐ **A** Some writing to describe needs to use a formal style.

☐ **B** Descriptive writing needs facts to make it believable.

☐ **C** Descriptive writing must start with the adverbial 'firstly'.

☐ **D** Headings and sub-headings must be used for reviews.

☐ **E** Reviews can use adjectives, similes or metaphors to describe.

Argue and persuade

Read the test-style task below and the information section on page 90. You don't need to complete it. Instead, think about what it is asking you to do.

> **TASK G**
>
> You have decided to take up the challenge and would like your friends to join you.
>
> Write an email to your friends, persuading them to take part in the Fitness Challenge.
>
> In your email you should:
>
> • give detailed reasons why your friends should take part in the challenge
> • explain exactly what the challenge involves
> • describe the benefits of taking part.

1   Persuasive writing needs to have key points backed up by evidence. Think of **two** key points and evidence you could use for the above task.

Point 1 and evidence ....

....

Point 2 and evidence ....

....

GUIDED 2   A counter-argument can be used to dismiss a reader's opposing point of view. How might a reader disagree with your points above? How might you be able to counter them? Write down your ideas.

> Evidence could take the form of facts, statistics, an expert opinion or an example from your own experience.

I realise that you might think ....

....

....

However, ...

....

3   You can also use language techniques to add power to your persuasion or argument. Which of the following techniques are useful when writing to persuade or argue? Circle your choices.

rhetorical questions   alliteration   lists   full stops   direct address

Audience

1   You will need to think carefully about the needs of your audience. Match up the statements below to the writing format.

Article   might have a wide audience but will depend on where it is going to appear

Review   needs to be factual and informative whoever it is intended for

Report   audience will usually be one specific person who can be addressed directly

Letter   audience depends on who reads the newspaper; for instance, if it is a community newspaper the audience may be both adults and children

Now read the test-style task below and the information section on page 88. You don't need to complete it. Instead, think about what it is asking you to do.

TASK E

You walk your dog in the woods and your children use the adventure playground. You decide to write a letter setting out your objections to the planning application. Write to Ms Tracey Bancroft, Head of Planning, Estrick Council, 3 Oak Lane, Estrick, BR2 5NG.

In your letter you should:

- state whether you agree or disagree with Estrick Council's proposals
- give detailed reasons to support your views
- state clearly what action you want Estrick Council to take.

> **GUIDED**

2   Which of the two options below has the most appropriate style and content for the audience in this task?
Put a cross in the box next to your choice.

> Always think carefully about what information your audience needs. Your letter will be more persuasive if you write about a variety of people who will be affected by the proposal.

☐ **A** Where will all the kids play? I'll need to go miles to walk my dog and my kids will be stuck inside all day.

☒ **B** I appreciate that the area needs more housing, but without the playground, children who are new to the area will have nowhere to play safely.

3   The second option uses a formal style and makes a strong point that is suited to the audience and purpose. Write **two** more sentences of this answer, using a formal style and making points that are suitable for the audience.

....

....

....

....

Formal writing

GUIDED   **1**   List **four** situations where you should use a formal style when writing.

You are applying for a job.

....

....

....

2   Which **three** of the following usually require a formal style? Circle your choices.

> Remember to read the writing task carefully and underline the audience, purpose and format. These will help you to decide which writing style to use.

letters   emails   articles   reports   reviews

3   Which **two** of the following are **not appropriate** for formal writing? Circle your choices.

slang   sentences   text language   punctuation   headings

Now read the test-style task below and the information section on page 87. You don't need to complete it. Instead, think about what it is asking you to do.

TASK D

You run a local charity that is in need of funds. You decide to apply for the charity grant on behalf of the charity. Write your letter of application to: Brian Edwards, Venture Volunteering, 4 Forest Lane, Burstone, BG1 4HH.

In your letter you should:

- describe the aims of your charity
- explain why you need the money
- describe exactly what difference the money could make to the local community.

---

4   A student has started an answer to the task above but has not used a formal style. Rewrite the start of the letter, using a formal style.

Dear Brian

I'm writing because I know you'll absolutely love my charity. We're the only charity here bothering to collect anything for kids with rare cancers.

....

....

....

....

Informal writing

GUIDED 1   List **three** situations where informal writing would be acceptable.

You are adding your own views to an informal discussion.

....

....

2   Emails can use an informal style, but which greeting is most suitable if you do not know the audience? Circle the correct answer.

Hi!   Dear Mr Smith   Hey!   Dear Sir or Madam

Look at the following test-style task. You don't have to complete it, just read it carefully and answer the questions that follow.

TASK G

You have decided to take up the challenge and would like your friends to join you. Write an email to your friends, persuading them to take part in the Fitness Challenge.

In your email you should:

• give detailed reasons why your friends should take part in the challenge
• explain exactly what the challenge involves
• describe the benefits of   taking part.

---

3   Which of the following would be suitable for the above task? Circle your choices.

contractions   informal phrases   text language   slang   complete sentences

4   A student has started an answer to the task above, but has used a style that is too formal for the audience. Rewrite it, using a more informal style.

Dear Friends

I am writing to tell you all about a challenge that has been advertised in the newspaper today. I think we would all benefit hugely from taking part in such a terrific fitness scheme.

In my view, we should all sign up for the outdoor boot camp. I am sure that, like me, you have started to put on weight since starting a desk job.

....

....

....

....

> If you use too many exclamation marks in your writing they will lose impact. A good rule is not to use more than two in a piece of writing.

Putting it into practice

In your writing test, you will need to show that you understand:

- the audience
- the purpose
- the type of text
- formal and informal texts.

Read the test-style task below and the information section on page 86. You don't need to complete it. Instead, think about what it is asking you to do.

TASK B

Write an article for your community newsletter.

In your article you may:

- describe the issue caused by the pedestrian-only zone
- explain what the long-term effects might be
- state what you think should be done about the issue.

---

1   Write the **first two** paragraphs of an answer, choosing a suitable title and sub-headings to match the purpose, format and audience.

Remember, before you start:
- underline the purpose, audience and format given in the task
- underline key words in the task.

....

....

....

....

....

....

....

....

....

....

....

....

....

Planning

1. Use the words below to fill in the blanks in the following instructions about how to plan a writing answer.

task	audience	information	ideas	bullet points

1. Read the task and the task .... carefully.

2. Identify .... , purpose and format.

3. Underline information in the .... that will help you with your answer.

4. Use the .... to structure your plan.

5. Use the information you have underlined in the task to add .... to your plan.

Now read this writing task and the task information on page 90. You don't have to answer it, just read it carefully, then answer the questions that follow.

TASK G

You have decided to take up the challenge and would like your friends to join you.
Write <u>an email to your friends</u>, persuading them to take part in the <u>Fitness Challenge</u>.

In your email you should:

- <u>give detailed reasons</u> why your friends should take part in the challenge
- <u>explain exactly</u> what the challenge involves
- <u>describe the benefits</u> of taking part.

---

 2. A student has started a plan for the above task by underlining key words and making notes about how to answer. Follow the steps above and complete the plan.

- Email to friends, can be informal.

- Subject heading: Let's get up off the couch!

- ....

- ....

- ....

- ....

> Notice how this plan has used some of the ideas from the task information on page 90. Always read the information carefully to get ideas.

Using detail

1   Which of these statements about planning is **not** true? Answer the question with **one** cross in the box you think is correct.

☐ **A**   You can use a spider diagram or a list for your plan.

☐ **B**   You can add ideas of your own to your plan.

☐ **C**   You must only use the information provided in the task.

☐ **D**   You should plan to use features that are suitable for the purpose.

☐ **E**   It is a good idea to follow the bullet points from the task.

2   Which **five** of the following should be included in your plan? Circle your choices.

a clear structure   an introduction   complete sentences

features for purpose   detail   statistics

Now read this writing task and the task information on page 93. You don't have to answer it, just read it carefully, then answer the questions that follow.

> **TASK J**
>
> Write the report for the Club committee meeting. In your report you should:
>
> - explain the problems the club has with membership
> - explain the advantages/disadvantages and costs of each option
> - suggest which you think   would be   best for the   club.

▷**GUIDED**▷ 3   A student has started a plan for the above task. Using your answers to questions 1 and 2 above, complete the plan. Remember to follow the steps from page 49.

> Notice that this plan uses a spider diagram, but a list or bullet points would work just as well. Make sure to number your points to give your writing a clear structure.

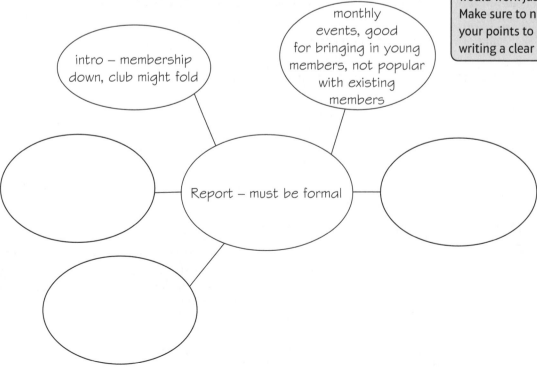

intro – membership down, club might fold

monthly events, good for bringing in young members, not popular with existing members

Report – must be formal

Paragraphs

1　Which **one** of the following statements about paragraphs is **not** true? Answer the question with **one** cross in the box you think is correct.

　☐　**A**　A paragraph is a group of sentences about one topic or idea.

　☐　**B**　Using paragraphs helps you to develop your ideas.

　☐　**C**　Paragraphs are an effective way of structuring your writing.

　☐　**D**　Paragraphs should be three sentences in length.

　☐　**E**　Similar ideas should be grouped together into paragraphs.

2　In your test, which **two** of the following formats should definitely be written in paragraphs? Circle your choices.

　articles　　　　emails　　　　adverts　　　　letters　　　　blog entries

3　Use the words below to fill in the blanks in the following instructions about using paragraphs.

develop	sentences	paragraph	topic	introduces	topic

　Each .... should start with a .... sentence. This is

　a sentence that clearly .... the reader to the content of the paragraph.

　The remaining .... in the paragraph should then be used to ....

　and add detail to the idea in the .... sentence.

GUIDED　4　A student has written the following planning notes for Task F on page 89. Structure them into a paragraph plan by grouping similar ideas into two separate paragraphs.

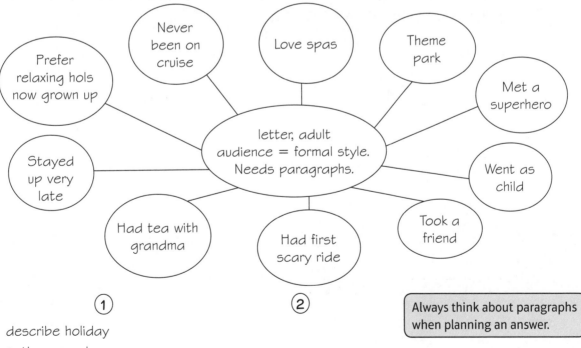

Always think about paragraphs when planning an answer.

describe holiday
- theme park
- went as child
- took a friend
- had first scary ride

Point–Evidence–Explain

1   Use the words below to complete the following rules for Point–Evidence–Explain paragraphs.

detail	sentence	details	evidence	explain	point

The first sentence should contain your .... After your point comes your

.... Evidence is .... This can be more than one ....

if you have a lot of .... to add. After your evidence you should ....

how the evidence backs up your point.

GUIDED   2   List **three** things you can use as evidence in your answers.

Facts

GUIDED   3   A student has written a P.E.E. paragraph for Task J on page 93, using some of the ideas from page 50. Label the point, the evidence and the explanation.

point

<u>One idea to bring in new members is to hold monthly event nights.</u> These could be talent

shows similar to those on TV at the moment as I know that they are very popular with young

people. I think they would also enjoy weekend discos and perhaps dancing lessons. This

could bring us new younger members who have not thought of joining a social club before.

4   Use P.E.E. to write another paragraph of an answer to Task J on page 93. Use some more of your ideas from your plan on page 50.

....

....

....

....

....

....

....

Linking ideas

> **GUIDED**   1   Copy the adverbials below into the table, adding each one to the correct column.

in addition	additionally	furthermore	~~for example~~
similarly	however	likewise	firstly
secondly	in the same way	in contrast	therefore
consequently	~~next~~	in conclusion	finally

Adding an idea	Explaining	Introducing evidence	Comparing and contrasting	Ordering points
		for example		next

Read Task Task E on page 88 carefully. You don't need to answer it. Just read it carefully and answer the questions below.

2   Complete one student's answer to the task. Fill in the gaps using appropriate adverbials.

..........................., I would like to state that I strongly disagree with Estrick Council's

proposals. ...., I think many local residents feel the same way.

Sharpness Woods is a well-known and well-loved local beauty spot. ...., many

families go for the day, taking a picnic and using the adventure playground. The playground

provides a safe area for children to play in the fresh air and it is the only outdoor play area

for several miles. Removing it would, ..., be a serious issue for local families.

3   Now write your own P.E.E. paragraph in response to the task on page 88. Use a range of adverbials to guide the reader through your ideas.

....

....

....

....

....

Putting it into practice

Read the test-style task below and the information on page 91.

TASK H

Write a report for your school/college/workplace on how to spend the technology budget.

In your report you should:

- explain what technology your school/college/workplace needs

- explain the advantages and disadvantages of each of the schemes

- make your recommendation   and give your reasons.

---

1   Use the space below to plan your answer
     to the task above.

> Remember to:
> - read the task carefully and underline key words
> - use the bullet points to structure your answer
> - use the information section and add your own ideas.

....

....

....

....

....

....

2   Now write **two** paragraphs of your answer. Focus on using clear P.E.E. paragraphs and
     appropriate adverbials.

....

....

....

....

....

....

....

Vocabulary

1   Synonyms are words with similar meanings. Complete the table by adding at least two synonyms for each word.

stop	sitting	getting

GUIDED 2   Look at each of the words in the table below. Complete the table by adding at least two more emotive alternatives for each word.

issue	think	bad	nice	take
	consider		terrific	

3   Now read part of a student's answer to Task G on page 90. Rewrite the answer, replacing the underlined words and phrases with more interesting vocabulary choices. Use some of those you found for questions 1 and 2 above.

We all need to accept that we have <u>an issue</u> with our weight. Please <u>take</u> some time <u>to think about</u> how we can <u>stop</u> ourselves from <u>sitting</u> for hours in front of the TV. Not only is this a really <u>bad</u> thing for our weight, but it is also <u>stopping</u> us <u>being with</u> our friends. Taking up a fitness challenge would help us to <u>get rid of the</u> weight, and I am sure you will agree that it would be <u>nice</u> to spend some time together.

....

....

....

....

....

....

....

> If you use a dictionary to find synonyms, make sure the word you use makes sense in your sentence. For instance, 'capture' is a synonym for 'take', but would not make sense in the paragraph above!

Language techniques 1

> **GUIDED** **1** Look at the extracts from students' writing below. Connect the language technique to the extract.

1 How would you feel if you had to park several streets away from your home?

Repetition

2 There was litter at the tram stop, there was litter on the floor of the tram and there was even litter on the seats.

3 We can't lose. The Boot Camp guarantee that if we try just one week of the fitness challenge we will be fitter.

Direct address

4 I felt incredibly dizzy after the waltzer and my stomach lurched as I realised I still had to face the helter skelter, the ghost train and the dodgems!

Lists

5 Just imagine how you will feel at the end of the challenge when you can fit back into your favourite jeans!

Rhetorical question

6 The main gains from following the fitness challenge include easier breathing, greater physical stamina and a slimmer waistline.

Now look at the test-style task below. You don't need to answer it. Instead, read it carefully, think about the language techniques above, then answer question 2.

TASK E

You walk your dog in the woods and your children use the adventure playground. You decide to write a letter setting out your objections to the planning application. Write to Ms Tracey Bancroft, Head of Planning, Estrick Council, 3 Oak Lane, Estrick, BR2 5NG.

In your letter you should:
• state whether you agree or disagree with Estrick Council's proposals
• give detailed reasons to support your views
• state clearly what action you want Estrick Council to take.

---

2 Write **two** short extracts of an answer to this task. Use **two** of the language techniques above.

....

....

....

....

....

....

....

Language techniques 2

GUIDED 1 Look at these examples of language techniques that are used to create images in readers' minds. Circle the technique that has been used in each sentence.

(a) Our greedy technology is gobbling up more of our time than ever.

alliteration   personification   simile   metaphor

(b) We have a mountain to climb if we want to get fit quickly!

alliteration   personification   simile   metaphor

(c) The trams were all dark, damp and dangerously slippery underfoot.

alliteration   personification   simile   metaphor

(d) I felt like an Arctic explorer when I slipped my skis on for the first time.

alliteration   personification   simile   metaphor

(e) I rushed towards the café like a desert explorer at an oasis.

alliteration   personification   (simile)   metaphor

(f) Sunlight danced on the water as I swam away from the shore.

alliteration   personification   simile   metaphor

Now look at the test-style task below. You don't need to answer it. Instead, read it carefully, thinking about the language techniques above. Then answer question 2.

TASK I

You visited the funfair on the first day. You decide to write a review of it for your weekly local newspaper.

In your review you could:
• describe the attractions at the funfair
• state what you enjoyed about the funfair
• suggest who might enjoy the funfair and why.

---

2 Write **two** short extracts of an answer to this task. Use **two** of the language techniques above.

....

....

....

....

....

....

Putting it into practice

You have now revised:

- choosing vocabulary for impact and effect

- using language techniques for impact and purpose.

Read the test-style task below and the task information on page 89. Write **two** paragraphs of an answer focusing on vocabulary choices and language techniques.

TASK F

Write an article for the *Broxtown Local News*, describing a memorable holiday in detail.

In your article you should:
- describe the holiday
- explain why it was memorable
- explain why you would enjoy the cruise.

> Remember, before you answer any question:
> - read the question carefully
> - underline key words about audience, purpose and format
> - spend five minutes writing a plan.

....

....

....

....

....

....

....

....

....

....

....

....

....

....

....

....

Sentences

1   All sentences need at least one verb. Underline the verbs in the sentences below.

   (a)   I will travel again by tram.   **(b)**   Simon will join me on the challenge.

   (c)   I walk to the gym every day.   **(d)**   Ben enjoyed the funfair.

   (e)   The pedestrian zone will help with traffic   **(f)**   Local residents walk in the woods.
        issues.

   (g)   The trams I went on all ran on time.

2   Every sentence needs a verb and someone or something to 'do' the verb. Look at the sentences in question 1 again and underline who or what is 'doing' the verb.

3   Extra detail can be added to sentences using the joining words *and, or, but, because*. Complete these sentences by adding extra detail or using a joining word.

   (a)   Ben enjoyed the funfair .... he felt it was too expensive.

   (b)   I walk to the gym every day .... it keeps me very fit.

   (c)   I will travel again by tram and ....

   (d)   Simon will join me on the fitness challenge but ....

⟩**GUIDED**⟩   4   The points in a sentence can be developed by using adverbials like *although, however, therefore, while, for example*. Develop **three** of the sentences from question 1 using **three** different adverbials from this list.

    The trams I went on all ran on time; however, they were not as clean as advertised.

    ....

    ....

    ....

    ....

5   Write **one** paragraph of an answer for the report task on page 93. Include **one** sentence with a joining word and **one** that is developed using an adverbial. You can use your plan from page 50.

    ....

    ....

    ....

    ....

    ....

Sentence variety

Read the test-style task below and the information on page 85. You don't need to answer it. Instead, think about what it is asking you to do and answer questions 1 and 2.

> **TASK A**
>
> Write an email to David, offering to help in one or more areas.
>
> In your email you should:
> * identify any group that interests you and explain why
> * describe what qualities or experience you have that make you suitable as a volunteer.

GUIDED 1 Write a sentence that you could use in your answer to the above task, beginning with each of the following word types.

A pronoun (*I, you, he, she, it, we, they*)

I have been involved with the book group for five years.

A preposition (*above, behind, between, near, with*)

....

An 'ing' verb (*walking, running, saying*)

....

An adjective (*large, tall, popular*)

....

An adverb (*quickly, importantly, interestingly*)

....

2 Now write a paragraph of an answer to the test-style task above. Aim to use at least **three** different types of sentence opening.

> Always think about the first word of your sentence. Varying the first word adds interest to your writing.

....

....

....

....

....

....

Writing about the present and future

 1 To write about the present, you need to think about the verb in your sentence. In each of the sentences below, circle the correct verb.

(a) We(hope)/hopes you consider/considers this matter urgently.

(b) I exercise/exercises regularly in the fresh air as part of the challenge.

(c) My friends at the gym encourages/encourage me to try harder.

(d) Jim loves/love the funfair and visit/visits regularly.

(e) Children play/plays in the woods and families walk/walks their dogs.

(f) People park/parks on the road as the town lacks/lack sufficient parking spaces.

2 Complete these sentences by adding a suitable verb in the present tense.

(a) I always .... football with my team on Saturdays.

(b) My book club .... very popular; we .... once a month.

(c) Our charity .... to help vulnerable children.

(d) I hope I .... the competition because I .... the idea of sailing on the high seas!

(e) Cars .... on the pavement, making it dangerous when we .... to school.

3 Change these sentences to the future tense by using *going to*.

(a) Ben runs every day in the park during the Fitness Challenge.

....

(b) I volunteer at the animal shelter every day in the summer.

....

(c) We are raising money for the hospital scanner appeal by swimming a mile.

....

4 You can also use *will* for the future tense. Write **three** sentences in the future tense using *will*.

....

....

....

Writing about the past

1   To write about the past, you need to think about the verbs in your sentences. Select the correct verb in these sentences to make them past tense.

   (a)   I applied/applyed/applying for the charity grant.

   (b)   Ellie and I complaind/complained/complain about the poor service on the tram.

   (c)   I filled/filling/fill in a complaint form about the state of the tram.

   (d)   My friends working/workd/worked hard on the Fitness Challenge.

   (e)   My friend park/parks/parked his car on the pavement.

   (f)   We have wasted/wastd/wasting opportunities to attract new members.

⟩**GUIDED**⟩ 2   Change these verbs to make each of the sentences past tense.

> Always think carefully about the verb in a sentence. If the present tense ends in -e, you can just add **-d** to make it past tense.

   (a)   John **try** ...._tried_.......... really hard to raise the money.

   (b)   I was so scared on the rollercoaster, I **cry**...........................!

   (c)   We **hurry** .... to finish our meal as the bistro was closing.

   (d)   The road is dangerous, so I **carry**........................... my daughter to our front gate.

3   Some verbs are tricky in the past tense. Circle the correct verb in each of these sentences.

   (a)   John done/did a half marathon during the Fitness Challenge.

   (b)   We are/were/was late for the fireworks at the funfair.

   (c)   I have/had/has an amazing time on holiday in Spain.

   (d)   I see/saw/seen many families walking in the woods last summer.

   (e)   I feel I have get/got/gets the right experience to volunteer.

   (f)   I ate/eat/eated at the hot dog stall.

   (g)   The Help a Neighbour scheme made/make/maked a real difference to my grandmother.

> Always check in a dictionary if you are unsure about a past tense verb. Practise any that you find tricky.

Putting it into practice

You have now revised:

- simple sentences
- adding detail to sentences
- varying your sentences
- writing in the past, present and future tenses.

Read the test-style task below and the information on page 85. Write **two** paragraphs of an answer in the space below. Make sure you:

- add detail to some of your sentences
- use linking words to join simple sentences
- use the correct tense throughout your answer.

TASK A

Write an email to David, offering to help in one or more areas.

In your email you should:
- identify any group that interests you and explain why
- describe what qualities or experience you have that make you suitable as a volunteer.

> Remember to plan your answer and include
> appropriate features for audience, purpose and format.

....

....

....

....

....

....

....

....

....

....

....

....

Full stops and capital letters

1   What should you use at the beginning of each sentence?

....

> **GUIDED**   2   List **three** reasons for using a capital letter.

for names like John Smith

....

....

3   How should you end a sentence if you want to suggest excitement or danger?

....

4   These sentences all contain two separate pieces of information. They also have some incorrect or missing capital letters. Rewrite them as **two** separate sentences, with full stops and the correct capital letters.

(a)   The charity fashion show starts at 8pm, mrs jones and her daughter janet will be providing the refreshments.

....

....

(b)   I think everybody should spend time exercising in the fresh air, my Friend pays far too much each month to go to a gym.

....

....

(c)   I had my Wedding at the broxtown social club, a jazz band plays there every saturday night.

....

....

5   These sentences all need some punctuation at the end. Add a full stop, a question mark or an exclamation mark.

(a)   Why should dog owners be forced to go miles into the countryside to exercise their pets

(b)   I was so scared on the rollercoaster I had to shut my eyes

(c)   I am not happy with the way you have handled my complaint about the tram

Commas

1   Look at the sentences below. Some use commas correctly and some do not. Tick the correct sentences and correct the incorrect ones.

Commas in a list

☐   Our charity is dedicated to helping carers and we can offer, financial support a day centre with a variety of activities and transport to and from hospital appointments.

☐   A pedestrian zone will ease parking issues, bring new trade to local shops and make the area safer for our children.

☐   Anybody can get fit on this challenge, it doesn't matter whether you are thin, tall, fat, short, young, or, old.

Commas to separate extra information

☐   Janet Hughes, a qualified personal trainer, oversees all the challenge programmes.

☐   The tram seats, which I would have liked to test for comfort had litter on them.

☐   Our profits which last year were over £500 are all dedicated to good causes.

GUIDED 2   Sometimes extra information is put at the start of the sentence. Rewrite the sentences below by moving the extra information to the start and adding a comma. Make sure capital letters are used correctly.

(a)   Pedestrian zones can help with parking problems if they are planned carefully.

....

(b)   I think I am well qualified to volunteer with a local community group as I have a lot of charity experience.

As I have a lot of charity experience, I think I am well qualified to volunteer with

a local community group.

(c)   Efforts should be made to keep the area free of housing as it is a popular local beauty spot.

....

3   Look at Task A on page 85 and write the first **three** sentences of a response. Use commas correctly to separate items in a list, and to add separate extra information within a sentence.

....

....

....

....

....

Apostrophes and inverted commas

1   Look at the sentences below. Some have used inverted commas correctly, and some have not. Tick the correct sentences and correct the incorrect ones.

> You can use either single or double inverted commas, but always remember to use them in pairs.

☐   Martin Hughes, a local resident, feels very strongly that the pedestrian area is a mistake, 'Shops will lose trade as people will not be able to park close to the shops'.

☐   Visitors to the funfair on a Saturday will be able to watch an open-air showing of Punch and Judy.

☐   Roll up, roll up! is the familiar cry from the funfair stalls.

☐   To help us on the challenge I have bought a copy of '21 days to fitness' by Joao Souza.

☐   I was described by my last employer as 'the safest pair of hands he had ever come across.

2   Add an apostrophe to **four** of the following sentences to show who owns what. One sentence does not need an apostrophe.

   (a)   My friends gym charges over £50 a month.

   (b)   The café at the funfair has a childrens menu.

   (c)   We are very proud of our charitys work.

   (d)   Friends of the Park is a really valuable community group.

   (e)   My schools sports facilities are the best in the city.

GUIDED   3   Rewrite the bold words in the sentences below as contractions by removing letters and replacing them with an apostrophe.

   (a)   **I do not** ....I don't......... think anybody is too old to start a fitness challenge.

   (b)   **I have** .... had enough of the council taking away our public spaces.

   (c)   **I am** .... not prepared to park my car miles from my house every day.

   (d)   I exercise regularly in the fresh air and **cannot** .... think of any better way to

   get fit.

   (e)   Running a group is something **I have** .... done before,

   so **I will** .... be able to help out straight away.

> Always think about your audience and format before using contractions – they are not suitable for formal writing

Spelling tips

1   The 'i' before 'e' rule helps you to remember the spelling of some difficult words. Use the rule to help you circle the correct spellings in the list below.

(a)   believe/beilieve/beleive

(b)   sceince/sceience/science

(c)   receive/recieve/reiceve

(d)   deiceive/deceive/decieve

(e)   reciept/reiceipt/receipt

(f)   friend/freind/frieind

2   Words with double letters can be difficult to spell. Circle the correct spellings in the list below.

(a)   address/adresse/addres

(b)   diferent/different/diferrent

(c)   tomorrow/tommorrow/tomorow

(d)   dissappoint/disappoint/disapoint

(e)   possible/posible/posibble

(f)   dissappear/disappear/disapear

(g)   embarrass/embarras/embarass

(h)   recomend/recommend/reccommend

GUIDED   **3**   A student is having trouble with words ending in **-ly** and words with silent letters. Correct the mistakes the student has made in these sentences.

(a)   The Council needs to take immediate action so that people can cross the road safley.

....

(b)   The tram driver even spoke to me very ~~rudley wen~~ I asked him to point out my stop.

> Very few words end in **-ley**. If you are unsure of a spelling, always check in a dictionary.

rudely when

(c)   Wen we start the challenge we can choose a course wich is best for our needs.

....

(d)   I am extremley concerned about the hole proposal for the pedestrian zone.

....

(e)   The funfair is haf price every Wenesday in the autum.

....

(f)   You should definetly try the hot dogs wen you visit.

....

Common spelling errors 1

There are common spelling errors that you can avoid in your writing. Some words sound the same but are spelled differently.

> there/their/they're
>
> to/too/two
>
> your/you're
>
> we're/wear/where/were
>
> of/off
>
> are/our

 1 Circle the correct spelling in each of the following sentences.

(a) I am happy to/too/two help with any of the projects as there/(they're)/their all good causes.

(b) I hope to/too/two be available to help for at least too/to/two hours each week.

(c) The challenge will be easy if we wear/where/we're comfortable clothes and listen to our/are favourite songs.

(d) Your/you're better of/off on the challenge, as joining a gym costs way to/too/two much money!

(e) Some passengers our/are very critical of/off the limited weekend tram timetable.

(f) We where/wear/were forced to change are/our holiday plans.

(g) There/they're/their not going to do anything about my complaint.

(h) There/their/they're are three reasons why your/you're plan will fail to/too/two solve the problem.

2 Complete these sentences with the correct spellings of the relevant words in question 1.

(a) Children .... at risk because people are parking .... cars on the pavement.

(b) We .... all able to ignore our health when we .... younger. Now

.... in .... forties we need to take .... health more seriously.

(c) .... not getting any younger so now is the time .... think about

.... health and fitness.

(d) You don't need to .... expensive gym gear to take part in the challenge.

(e) .... is no reason .... pay expensive gym fees when you can exercise

outside for nothing.

(f) .... health is .... important to be ignored.

> Every time you use one of these words, stop and think about the spelling.

Common spelling errors 2

GUIDED **1** Circle the correct word in each of the following sentences.

(a) The Council (should have)/should of done something about the parking problem in town.

(b) You could of/could have saved money if you had brought/bought a family ticket.

(c) I brought/bought my own tennis racquet to the challenge but could of/could have used the ones provided by the instructor.

(d) I no/know/now that the Council takes this type of problem seriously.

(e) I'll write/right to you all again as soon as I have the right/write information.

(f) Considering the amount of opposition to the plans, the Council should of/should have brought/bought this matter to our attention earlier.

2 Complete these sentences using the correct versions of the words in the list below.

> would have/could have/should have
>
> bought/brought
>
> write/right
>
> know/no/now

(a) My friend .... his family to the funfair .... after it opened.

(b) A lot of issues .... been prevented if the Council had taken action.

(c) Surely you .... how strongly local residents feel about this issue?

(d) We feel that local residents should definitely .... been involved in the planning process.

(e) The charity could not .... survived without the .... type of volunteer.

(f) Exercising on my own .... been really tough without the .... music to keep me motivated.

(g) There is .... reason for any of the trams to be dirty; they ....

.... been cleaned every day.

(h) If we start .... away we could be fit by Christmas!

(i) Joining the challenge will be a great way to use the bike you .... last month.

> Leave time at the end of your writing tasks to check
> your work. Make sure all your sentences make sense.

Common spelling errors 3

> **GUIDED** 1   Some of the most frequently misspelled words are in the table below. In each row, one spelling is correct and two are incorrect. Tick the correct spelling and cross out the incorrect spellings.

explanation	exsplanashun	exsplanation
~~feirce~~	~~fierse~~	fierce ✓
althoght	although	allthough
becuse	becos	because
decide	deside	dicide
arguement	argument	argumant
hapened	happend	happened
bewtiful	beautiful	butiful
interrupt	interupt	intterupt
bisiness	busness	business
menwhile	meanwhile	meenwhile
separate	seperate	seprate
unfortunatly	unfortunately	unfortunitly
queue	que	quew
remembre	remember	remembur
perswade	persade	persuade
straight	strate	strait
preparation	preperation	preperashun
nervus	nervous	nervos
autumn	autum	awtum
achually	achully	actually

2   Now check your answers on page 70 of the Revision Guide. Use the space below to practise any spellings you are unsure of.

> Every time you spell a word incorrectly, make a note of it and practise the correct spelling regularly.

Plurals

1   Follow the rules to make the **bold** words in these sentences into plurals.

(a)   Before the fitness challenge you are given a range of fitness **test**. ....

(b)   Several of our local **church** .... use volunteers to do the flower displays.

(c)   It is easier to use the trams as our **bus** .... are all overcrowded.

(d)   If you had nine **life**, ... then you could afford to ignore your health.

(e)   It was very hot today; I drank four **glass** .... of water.

(f)   One of the main attractions of the funfair is the big **box** .... of sweets you can win!

(g)   I will not stop until the Council abolishes its **plan** .... for the pedestrian zone.

(h)   We have only **ourself** .... to blame if we do not act now.

GUIDED **2**   When words end in **y**, you need to look at the letter before the **y** before creating the plural. Circle the correct plural in these sentences.

(a)   The funfair is lovely in the evenings, but the (flies)/flys are annoying.

(b)   Those with family/families need to remember that the funfair has no changing area for babys/babies.

(c)   Even in the middle of big citys/cities you can find a park to exercise in.

(d)   Many local librarys/libraries have activitys/activities for children.

(e)   Parking restrictions should be in place on Sundays/Sundaies.

(f)   Large parties/partys can get a discount on weekdays/weekdaies.

3   Some words become different words when they are plural. Circle the plurals in the sentences below.

(a)   All child/children should be accompanied by an adult.

(b)   A lot of person/people walk their dogs in the woods.

(c)   Most men/man I know prefer to exercise at a gym.

(d)   Most of the volunteers are woman/women, but more man/men are joining.

(e)   I find dancing difficult as I think I have two left foot/feet!

Checking your work

 1 Look at this extract from a student's writing. Circle and correct all the errors you can find. Look for any errors in:

- spelling

- punctuation

- tense

- sentences, for example misused or repeated words or incomplete sentences.

A fitness challenge is just what we need to get rid of ⟨are⟩ *our* winter flab. We all now that we

shouldn't of had all those crisps and fizzy drinks while slumped in front off the TV!

Challenging ourselfs to a series of boot camp sessions in the open air wud be a really

brilliant idea. Instead of watching yet another box set we culd experiance the great

outdoors get fit and lose weight. Fitness4u have fully qualifyed personal trainers who

will look after us every step off the way. You need not be nervus about injurys as they

garantee to measure are fitness throughout the programme.

2 You should always check your work. Go back over your longer answers in this workbook and see if you have made any errors like those in question 1 above. Use the table below to list any errors you have made.

Spelling errors	Punctuation errors	Sentence errors

> Use the completed table to see what types of mistake you make regularly. Look out for them when you check your written work during the test.

Putting it into practice

You have now revised:

- punctuation
- spelling
- checking your work.

Read Task C on page 86. Answer the task and check your work carefully when you have finished. Pay particular attention to the types of mistake you identified on page 72.

> Remember to spend:
> - 5 minutes planning (use the task information and bullet points)
> - 20–23 minutes writing and checking (leave at least 2 minutes to read through and correct any mistakes).

Putting it into practice (example answer)

Look at a student's answer to Task D (page 87). Read the comments to see why the student has passed the Functional Skills Level 2 Writing test. Rewrite the student's answer on a separate sheet of paper, making the improvements suggested below.

Dear Mr Edwards

I am writing to apply for the £10,000 charity grant that your company makes available each year to a local charity.

My charity, Little Stars, has been helping children in this area for over 16 years. Our main aim is to support children who have a sporting ambition but lack the money to get their dreams. We provide coaching, equipment, kit and transport to help talented youngsters get to their full potential.

Over the last year we have publicised our charity. We have used social media sites. We are now getting a lot more interest. Whilst this is exciting it means that we often can't help every child that applys for funds.

Your grant would be very useful. Many local childrens' lives have been transformed by our support. For example, James Finch is now playing with the Burstone Football Academy and Jenny Black is training with the England Lady's hockey team.

We are all very enthusiastic and work extremely hard to help all the children who come to us for help. Please give serious thought to helping us.

Yours sincerely

Janet Chester

What has been done well:

- ✓ Format is correct for a letter.
- ✓ The bullet points from the task and the information section have been used to plan the answer.
- ✓ The letter has clear paragraphs that have been developed with relevant details.
- ✓ Spelling is accurate.
- ✓ The student has used commas correctly in a list.
- ✓ Specific vocabulary has been used for impact 'transformed', 'enthusiastic', 'extremely'.
- ✓ The tone is mostly formal and appropriate for the audience and purpose.

What could be improved:

- ✗ The word 'get' is repeated in the second paragraph and could be replaced with more emotive synonyms.
- ✗ Some of the sentences are too short and could be joined.
- ✗ Some plurals are incorrect, such as 'Lady's'.
- ✗ Some possessive apostrophes are incorrect, such as 'childrens''.

Putting it into practice (example answer)

Look at a student's answer to Task I (page 92). Read the comments to see why the student has failed the Functional Skills Level 2 Writing test. Rewrite the student's answer on a separate sheet of paper, making the improvements suggested below.

Fanciful Fun Fair

Rides
I visited the fun fair last night and had a wicked time! First I went on the dodgems, then the waltzers and the gost train. Whilst the gost train was OK it was not really that scary so I was a bit dissapointed.

Food
I ate loads! The Jamaica food was great realy tasty filing, and quite cheap. Although I would have liked more! I went with a freind and he eat so many hot dogs I thought he were going to pop!

Who would like it
My kids loved the fair and done everything including the helter skelter which is great for kids so your kids would love it. Its great for familys.

What has been done well:

✓ Some attempt has been made to use the bullet points and the information from the task.

✓ Headings and sub-headings are suitable for the format and purpose.

✓ Some attempt has been made to use a variety of sentences.

✓ Some adverbials have been used.

What needs to be improved:

✗ The heading and the sub-headings are not interesting enough for a newspaper review.

✗ The style is not formal enough for a newspaper article. 'OK' is too informal.

✗ The language does not suit the purpose, it is not exciting enough for a review. The words 'kids' and 'great' are repeated too often.

✗ There are some spelling errors, particularly with double letter words.

✗ There are some mistakes with tenses.

✗ The final sentence is missing an apostrophe and it has an incorrect plural.

> Some of the words that were in the task information have been misspelled here. Always copy the information carefully and check your spelling at the end.

TEXT A

Cycling – an Olympic legacy?

Cycling has become remarkably popular over the last four years. According to a new report, sales of bikes have increased by 20% per year since 2012. Many people credit this renewed love of the bicycle to the 'Wiggo Effect', named after Bradley Wiggins, one of the cyclists in the incredibly successful British team in the 2012 Olympics.

More people than ever are joining cycling clubs, with participation in competitive events increasing by a whopping 130% over the last four years. The government's cycle to work scheme has also seen a surge in interest, up more than 30% in 2013 alone. All of those taking part pay less tax, as well as saving on petrol.

Unfortunately, recent research shows that overall bicycle use across the country has remained static, bringing into question the success of the so-called 'Wiggo Effect' in getting more people cycling more often. Cycling still accounts for just 2% of all journeys across the country, a figure which has remained unchanged since 2012.

This is a shame as the report, published this week on our website, suggests that 90% of those who take up cycling notice some form of health benefit. According to one expert we interviewed, 'Cycling provides an excellent all-round workout and, as it is low impact, it is great for those wanting to take up a sport later in life.'

Amazingly, the report also suggests that cycling can benefit even those who are too welded to their couch to ever consider pushing the pedals. Shifting just 10% of journeys from car to bike would reduce air pollution enough to prevent 100 premature deaths each year. If more of us were pedal pushers we could cycle our way to the Danish model, where 20% of journeys are by bike. Doing this could make the country fit enough to save the NHS a staggering £17 billion over the next 20 years.

So, maybe we should all think back to that golden Olympic month when Britain seemed to rule the world on two wheels. It seems we'd all be fitter, healthier and richer on two wheels.

TEXT B

Cycle your way to health

Cycling is one the best ways to get more active, and can be enjoyed safely by people of all ages from all walks of life.

Cycling can easily be incorporated into your daily life. You can cycle to school, to work, to the shops, or just ride for fun. Adults should do at least 150 minutes of moderate activity each week. Children and young people should attempt 60 minutes of vigorous activity every day. 30 minutes of cycling, which raises your heart-beat and increases your breathing, counts towards these recommended activity targets.

Before you start

1. For short journeys, any good bike will do. If you buy second-hand, consider taking the bike to a specialist shop for servicing before you ride it.

2. Buy a helmet. It is estimated that 60% of cycling deaths could be prevented by wearing an approved safety helmet. Look out for the BSI safety kite mark to make sure the helmet you buy has passed all safety testing. If you have children, get them into the habit of wearing a helmet as soon as they start cycling, even when riding with stabilisers.

3. Consider taking part in a cycle training scheme. Your local Council or bike shop should be able to tell you about local cycling courses. Safety awareness courses are available for children and for adults who are new to cycling.

4. Before you start cycling in traffic, check the Highway Code for up-to-date rules and regulations for cyclists.

5. Wear reflective clothing, particularly in the winter months. If you don't want to wear a bright, fluorescent jacket, try reflective armbands.

6. Get a small repair kit and keep it on your bike at all times. Getting a puncture when miles from home in the pouring rain is never fun, but it is easier to deal with if you have a repair kit with you.

Staying motivated

There are many wonderful places to cycle in cities and the countryside is usually close enough for most cyclists to get to on a day trip. Think about signing up for a group bike ride. It's a great way to stay motivated and experience the great outdoors. You can be sponsored for your favourite charity, or simply join a cycling club that organises regular rides in your local area.

TEXT C

Cyclist vs Driver: a war coming soon to a city near you

In Toronto, they've painted over the cycle lanes. It's not because the streets are unsafe for cyclists. It's not because cars can no longer find space on roads heaving with over-zealous Olympic hopefuls. It's because the car drivers of Toronto are so strongly anti-bike that aggressive behaviour towards cyclists is common.

It isn't just in Toronto that car drivers have declared war on cyclists. Here in England feelings are beginning to run high against those on two wheels, particularly since the government announced new plans to spend even more money making our major cities more cycle friendly.

So what exactly do car drivers hold against their two-wheeled enemies?

Well, for one, cyclists do not pay road tax and do not have to register their vehicle. This means that all those shiny new bike lanes have actually been paid for by car drivers, not by the cyclists themselves. If a car driver ignores a red light, his registration number can be used to trace and fine him. The same cannot be done if a cyclist breaks the law.

It isn't just cyclists ignoring red lights that annoys those in cars. Cyclists are seen as breaking many of the rules of the road, such as overtaking on both sides of cars, cutting corners, riding on pavements and riding two abreast on narrow roads. The most annoying habit of cyclists, according to David Evans, of the organisation Safety First, is failing to use hand signals when cycling in traffic.

'Car drivers would be fined, or at least seriously warned, if they failed to use their indicators or lights. So why should those who pay nothing to use the roads be treated differently? It is often cyclists behaving irresponsibly who cause serious accidents, but it is usually the car driver who bears the cost.'

Evans does agree that cycling should be encouraged as it is undoubtedly better for our health than sitting in a car. But cyclists be warned – the health benefits do not make you king of the road. Evans wants a tax introduced on cycling to match the tax paid for cars, and also a compulsory test for cyclists: 'At the very least, cyclists should read the Highway Code, particularly if they are thinking of riding to work in heavy traffic.'

TEXT D

Fast Fashion

How often do you shop for clothes? Monthly? Weekly? Some people might be surprised to hear that many young people browse for fashion on a daily basis. A new study suggests that women under the age of 25 have five times more clothes in their wardrobe than women of their age group in 1980.

Recent stories about poor working conditions in overseas factories do not seem to have dented sales of cheap fashion. The study reports that most UK retailers now use large, modern factories that are thoroughly inspected on a regular basis. Many have also signed up to a charter that sets wages at a basic minimum and allows workers access to decent living conditions.

So, even if you prefer top-end classics that you keep for years, you can accessorise these with fast fashion to change your look every season.

These factories mean that high-street clothing stores have mastered the art of 'fast fashion'. They can put copies of catwalk creations into their stores quickly, easily and very cheaply. In fact, some stores are able to sell designer lookalikes for less than the price of a takeaway for two.

Gaynor Smith has taken this fast-fashion purchasing even further. 'It makes me laugh when people say they've spent £50 on an outfit. I'll never go above £6.' In order to keep up to date with trends, value fashion stores need to get rid of unsold stock on a regular basis. According to Gaynor, you just need to play the game: 'I watch things being reduced and when they reach the price I want to pay, I swoop.'

All this fast-fashion shopping has had an unexpected knock-on benefit for the charity sector. It seems we all love to rummage through other people's cast-offs as charity store sales are now booming, with many reporting increases in sales of over 100% in the last year alone. This is good news for the environment as it stops all our unwanted clothes from being dumped into overcrowded landfill sites.

TEXT E

How to look good on a budget

Rich people have it easy, don't they? Not only do they have everything they need, but they get to look amazing as well.

When something catches their eye, they just throw a wad of money at it, without ever bothering to look at the price tag. If they're unsure about what suits them, they have personal stylists to tell them what looks good and what doesn't. If they don't like something when they take it home, they can just leave it in the bag.

If only you had their money, their bank accounts, their credit cards. You'd be looking just as good. Better, even.

Luckily, you don't have to spend loads of money to look stylish. You can tighten the purse strings and still dress well, if you follow our five simple rules.

1. Shop during sales. As clothes shops now change their stock on a monthly basis, there is always a sale of some sort on somewhere. Expensive, classic items are the best things to buy in sales, but be careful to only buy what you actually need. A recent survey found that the average Briton wastes £140 every year buying sales items they never wear!

2. Buy from charity shops. Don't be afraid to root around and take your time. Dive into those tubs of scarves and bags and hats. When you find something wonderful, congratulate yourself. You'll be helping the environment as well as donating to a good cause, as charity shopping stops piles of clothes being dumped into landfill sites.

3. Invest in a few timeless classics, such as black trousers and a black jacket. By adding inexpensive accessories, or items you have found in a sale, you can put together several different outfits.

4. Sell, or swap, clothes that you don't wear any more. It's much more environmentally friendly than just dumping them in the bin. There are several online sites specialising in second-hand clothing, and it's easy to take a picture of the clothes on your phone. If you don't want to sell, you could invite friends round for regular swapping parties. One friend's expensive mistake could be your new little black dress.

5. Get creative, and learn to make your own clothes. Look around at what other people are wearing and then create your own style. Many colleges run dressmaking courses, and there are loads of easy-to-follow videos online.

TEXT F

How cheap are our cheap clothes?

Buying cheap clothing is ridiculously easy these days, thanks to fast-fashion labels.

But what is the real cost of the rails of cheap clothes we seem unable to do without? A recent study examines the working practices of the top fast-fashion brands, and shines a light on just how unethical they really are.

The only way to produce enough stock to satisfy our demand for cheap clothing is to manufacture it overseas. While recent horror stories about the use of child labour have stopped many of the worst abuses in overseas factories, there is no doubt that conditions are still way below the standards that would have to be adopted in factories in the UK.

'In the washing room there are lots of chemicals and the ceiling is not high, so it gets very hot and stuffy,' said one woman, who asked not to be named. As many as 600 workers in the women's factory were crammed into a low-ceilinged, window-less room for over eight hours without a break. 'When the inspectors come, they are only taken to the best parts of the factory.'

Many of these workers sleep nearby in employee housing that is owned and managed by their employer, and the conditions are just as bad there. Bare stone floors, no running water and a lack of toilet facilities are all common. Sometimes accommodation is simply wooden huts with three or four people to a room. They are simply not paid enough to find suitable alternative housing.

It may not have occurred to you that such horrific conditions are the true cost of your thrifty fashion bargains. After all, Fairtrade chocolate and other ethically produced foods are now firmly on the radar of most people and stocked in even the smallest of supermarkets. If you want to source similarly ethical fashion, however, you might find it a little more difficult.

A few top fashion brands actively advertise that they do not use any overseas factories that use 'sweatshop' style labour. But they tend to be the top end, designer label brands. However, if we want to help improve working conditions overseas and help the environment, perhaps we might be better off shopping for rich people's cast-offs in charity shops. That way, your money goes to a good cause, not to a company that treats its employees like cattle.

TEXT G

SUPERFOODS FOR FAMILY HEALTH

I understand that many readers will be tempted by articles promising to help them slash pounds from their food shop. Such articles are often impossible to ignore, particularly when we are on a tight budget and have a family to feed. But be careful – eating cheaply can mean missing out on vital healthy nutrients.

To keep your family healthy, you should plan to eat nutritional superfoods on a regular basis. It might cost a bit more, but it's really easy to add nutrient-rich, tasty foods to your weekly menus and create delicious feasts that not only taste amazing, but will also bring long-term health benefits.

A recent study by a leading university found that many superfoods such as salmon, avocado and coconut oil can help your body to get rid of harmful waste products. Dan Streeter, the professor who led the study, explains: 'This can help you recover after injury, lower your blood pressure and even improve your short-term memory.'

Streeter also feels that vitamin and mineral supplements are helpful to the modern family. Most of us know that eating our five portions of fruit and veg a day helps to keep us healthy, but Streeter warns that going without meat or fish on a regular basis can leave some people short on essential vitamins and minerals.

'Superfoods are available in capsule form from every supermarket these days. Even if you eat a diet high in vegetables, it is wise to add a vitamin supplement to counteract the effects of modern life such as stress, pollution and lack of sunlight.'

TEXT H

SHOPPING FOR LESS

The cost of living is creeping up again, so it's impossible to cut down any more on household bills. Food is just so expensive now, and cutting corners leads to unhealthy food choices.

Wrong! It's all about careful planning and sensible shopping.

Money experts say it's actually possible to slash your shopping bills by as much as half, without resorting to a diet of unhealthy frozen pizza. A lot of what we buy each week is wasted as either we don't eat it in time, or we decide when we get it home that we don't actually need it. We are also wasting money on 'healthy' supplements that we don't even need.

So what simple steps can we take to stay healthy and significantly reduce our shopping bills?

1.   Take a list to the shops. Plan your meals for the week in advance, shop once and buy only what you need. Keep essentials like bread in the freezer so you don't feel tempted to shop too often.

2.   Go vegetarian for at least one meal a week. Buying seasonal vegetables and adding pulses rather than meat to your stews and casseroles is cheaper, and it's much healthier than eating too much expensive meat.

3.   Buy single items where possible, particularly if you only cook for one. Why buy a big bag of carrots to rot in the fridge when you only need one?

4.   Don't buy expensive vitamin or health-food supplements. A balanced diet will give you all the vitamins you need.

5.   Don't feel you need to buy the latest 'superfood'. Fresh fruit and vegetables are the only 'superfoods' you need. Avoiding fast food and eating at least five portions of fruit and veg a day are the best ways to stay healthy.

6.   Beware of 'buy one get one free' offers. That free punnet of strawberries might seem tempting in the shop, but if you live on your own you'll have to eat a lot every day to finish them before they go off!

7.   Home-made sauces cost at least a third less than sauces in jars. Learn to cook and find recipes for simple pasta, curry and chilli dishes and batch cook them from scratch. You can then freeze portions to use when you're short of time.

TEXT I

IS IT POSSIBLE TO EAT FOR £12 A WEEK?

It's mealtime in a typical family home. Two younger children are eating chicken nuggets and chips, a teenager is eating a pasta ready meal and the adults are tucking in to a takeaway curry. The total cost is £35.

According to a leading family-support charity, the average UK family now spends more on ready meals, restaurant dining and takeaways than they spend on food for meal preparation. This is leading to a debt mountain for many families, says Tom Brown, Director of the charity Familycrisis.

However, Brown feels that there is an alternative to this debt crisis: 'With careful planning, an adult can eat for as little as £12 and still have a healthy, balanced diet.'

To do this, families would have to eat every meal at home. So no more chicken nuggets, frozen chips or takeaways. No more splashing out on Sunday lunch at your local pub.

Brown recommends replacing convenience foods with starchy foods like baked potatoes, and eating more vegetarian meals using healthy fruit and vegetables such as cabbage, cauliflower and tinned tomatoes. Pasta is a good mid-week option, but Brown says the sauce must be home-made: 'Any sauce in a jar is going to cost more than home-made sauces, as well as being stuffed full of unnecessary sugar and salt.'

The problem with Brown's ideas is that people no longer have the cooking skills that allowed our grandparents to cook from scratch every day. My grandmother would spend hours scouring the supermarket shelves for bargains. When she got her shopping home, not a scrap was wasted.

To Tom Brown the answer is simple. 'Take a cookery course. Shop carefully and squeeze every last penny out of your household shop.' So, to cut down on that food bill it might be time to live like your grandmother and learn to love your oven.

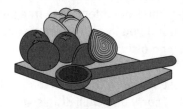

TASK A

Information
You read the following advert on a social networking site.

Do you want to give something back to your local community?

Volunteers are needed for the following local community groups:

- Help a Neighbour – this group provides neighbourhood help to the elderly with shopping, gardening and hospital visits. They need volunteer drivers and somebody to help out with administration.

- Library Reading Group – a group that meets monthly in the library. The group needs help with publicity and refreshments.

- Under-10s football club – the club desperately needs a new coach as well as people to help out with transport to away games.

- Girls' netball team – the team has just started and trains weekly at the Sports Centre. Volunteers would be welcome to help with coaching, publicity and administration.

- Friends of the Park – a group that meets weekly at the park to help maintain the grounds. Any help with gardening and decorating of the pavilion would be much appreciated.

Any skills or previous experience would be very welcome but are not essential. If you have enthusiasm and spare time, we will be able to find something for you to do!

If you are interested, email david@example.com

Writing task
Write an email to David, offering to help in one or more areas.
In your email you should:
- identify any group that interests you and explain why
- describe what qualities or experience you have that make you suitable as a volunteer.

You may include any other information.

TASK B

Information

Recently your local council agreed plans to make your town centre a pedestrian-only zone. This has led to serious traffic congestion and parking problems in the streets just outside this area. You decide to write an article for your community newsletter about this issue.

You make the following notes:

- There are not enough car parking spaces on the outskirts of town.
- Cars are being parked dangerously on the pavement.
- Residents cannot now park outside their own houses.
- Shops in the town are suffering as people can't park.
- Emergency vehicles find it difficult to get into the centre of town.
- Shops are unable to take deliveries except in the very early hours.

Writing task

Write an article for your community newsletter. In your article you may:
- describe the issue caused by the pedestrian-only zone
- explain what the long-term effects might be
- state what you think should be done about the issue.

You may include any other ideas.

TASK C

Information

You read the following advertisement in your local community newspaper.

New Burstone Tram Route opened!

All our trams are brand new, clean and ultra-reliable!

We can promise:
- 99% of our trams run on time
- our drivers are always friendly, courteous and helpful
- our tram stops are clean, safe and well-lit.

Best of all – if you are heading off to see one of the many other highly anticipated events in Burstone this summer, you can get discounted travel on the new tram route! We can guarantee that our discounts mean we are the cheapest way to get around town.

Writing task

You have bought a monthly season ticket and use the new tram route on a regular basis. You are pleased with most aspects of the service, but there have been some problems. You decide to write a review of the tram service for *The Burstone Weekly*.

In your review you should:
- state what is good about the tram service
- describe what the problems are
- suggest what improvements could be made.

TASK D

Information
You read the following advertisement in your local newspaper.

£10,000 grant available to local charity group!

The Venture Volunteering Company has been working with local charities for over 60 years, providing opportunities for people to travel abroad and help a charity of their choice.

We use all of our profits to help charitable causes, and award £10,000 each year to a local charity that we feel most deserves our support.

Are you a local charity desperately in need of funds?

Can you persuade us that £10,000 will make a real difference in your local community?

Have you got the drive and energy to make the money really work for your charity?

If you answered 'yes' to these questions, apply immediately and give us full details of your charity. Try to excite our judges by describing what you will be able to achieve with the money.

Writing task
You run a local charity that is in need of funds. You decide to apply for the charity grant on behalf of the charity. Write your letter of application to: Brian Edwards, Venture Volunteering, 4 Forest Lane, Burstone, BG1 4HH.

In your letter you should:
- describe the aims of your charity
- explain why you need the money
- describe exactly what difference the money could make to the local community.

TASK E

Information

You read the following on your local Council's noticeboard.

Estrick Council

Sharpness Woods

Estrick Council announce that a planning application is to be considered with regard to Sharpness Woods and the Sharpness Adventure Playground site. This application will be for the sale of the land for the development of houses and retail premises.

Comments on the application will be heard at a public meeting to be held in August. Those wishing to speak at the meeting should submit their comments in writing to the Council no later than 31 July.

Submit your objections to Ms Tracey Bancroft, Head of Planning, Estrick Council, 3 Oak Lane, Estrick, BR2 5NG.

Writing task

You walk your dog in the woods and your children use the adventure playground. You decide to write a letter setting out your objections to the planning application. Write to Ms Tracey Bancroft, Head of Planning, Estrick Council, 3 Oak Lane, Estrick, BR2 5NG.

In your letter you should:
- state whether you agree or disagree with Estrick Council's proposals
- give detailed reasons to support your views
- state clearly what action you want Estrick Council to take.

TASK F

Information

You read the following in the *Broxtown Local News*.

Holiday of a lifetime competition!

How would you like to sail away on a luxury liner and leave all your worries behind for fourteen wonderful nights?

We are offering four lucky readers the opportunity to win an all-inclusive cruise aboard the brand-new *Atlantis Princess*. Twelve decks of sheer indulgence await you. The Princess boasts three pools, six bars, five restaurants, a spa and a theatre showing top West End shows every night. Not only will you not have to pay for anything on board, you will also have £500 to spend on excursions.

To win your place on the *Princess*' maiden voyage around the Mediterranean, all you have to do is tell us about your most memorable holiday and why you deserve a cruise. Good or bad, home or abroad – it doesn't matter. You just need to entertain our readers!

The best tales will be published every Monday for the next two months, when readers will be given the chance to vote for their four favourites.

Writing task

Write an article for the *Broxtown Local News*, describing a memorable holiday in detail.

In your article you should:
• describe the holiday
• explain why it was memorable
• explain why you would enjoy the cruise.

TASK G

Information
You read the following advertisement on a national newspaper's website.

Fitness Challenge

Do you need to lose weight? Do you want to get fit so that you can run around with your children? Do you long to run a marathon but have no idea where to start? Or are you a couch-potato who needs to put down the remote control and get active?

If so, don't worry! At Fitness4u we have set up a series of monthly challenges to help you reach your fitness goal. You can choose from the following:

*   Hard-core boot camps in the open air
*   Gentle stretching classes for those new to exercise
*   'Couch 2 Parkrun' sessions as an introduction to jogging
*   Dance classes for those who want to dance their way to fitness
*   Nordic walking classes – the new fitness craze that allows you to socialise while you walk

At the start of each session of classes you will be weighed and your overall fitness measured by our professional fitness coaches. You will then be helped to set an achievable target before starting your four-week course.

We are so confident that you will reach your goal that we offer a money-back guarantee!

To help you keep on track, you will become part of an online community where you can swap tips, get encouragement and post details of your success.

Writing task
You have decided to take up the challenge and would like your friends to join you.
Write an email to your friends, persuading them to take part in the Fitness Challenge.

In your email you should:
*   give detailed reasons why your friends should take part in the challenge
*   explain exactly what the challenge involves
*   describe the benefits of taking part.

TASK H

Information

You read this on a noticeboard at your school/college/workplace.

Technology Budget

We have put aside £20,000 to upgrade our technology.

We are considering two schemes:

- Installing a new computerised appointments system for reception, which would include screening and registration of all visitors.
- Purchasing of electronic signage outside and inside the building, to include a large-screen display in the reception area to showcase our work.

The budget will only cover one of the above schemes, so we would like you to investigate the benefits of each one and report back with a recommendation.

Writing task

Write a report for your school/college/workplace on how to spend the technology budget. In your report you should:

- explain what technology your school/college/workplace needs
- explain the advantages and disadvantages of each of the schemes
- make your recommendation and give your reasons.

TASK I

Information
You read the following in your local newspaper.

FANCIFUL FUNFAIR
COMES TO ESTRICK!

Open daily
in the Estrick Pleasure Gardens for the whole of May

The largest funfair in the South West
makes its annual visit to our town!

All the usual attractions are back:
Dodgems
Waltzers
Helter Skelter
Ghost Train
Plus loads more!
New this year is an International Food Court, featuring stalls with the following cuisines:
Jamaican
Spanish Tapas
American Hot Dogs
Indian
Chinese
Italian Pasta Bar

Open 10am – 11pm

You visited the funfair on the first day. You decide to write a review of it for your weekly local newspaper.

In your review you could:
* describe the attractions at the funfair
* state what you enjoyed about the funfair
* suggest who might enjoy the funfair and why.

TASK J

Information

You are on the committee for your local social club and receive the following email from the Club Secretary.

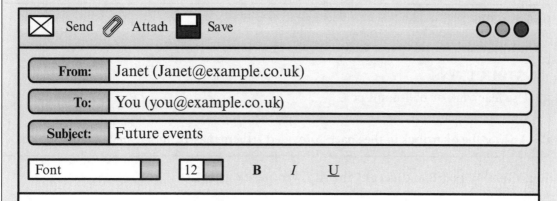

✉ Send	📎 Attach	💾 Save	○ ○ ●

From: Janet (Janet@example.co.uk)

To: You (you@example.co.uk)

Subject: Future events

Font   12   **B**   *I*   <u>U</u>

Hi

We have some really important decisions to make! We have lost a third of our members over the last five years and need to do something urgently to stop the club folding altogether. As you know, we surveyed the membership to ask people which activities would tempt them to attend more often. The following four were the most popular:

- Holding 'The Club's Got Talent' events monthly
- Hiring a big screen and showing sporting events and films each week
- Inviting guest speakers to club nights

Can you put together a report about the three options so that we can discuss them at the committee meeting next week? We'll need an idea of the benefits/disadvantages and the costs of each.

Thanks
Janet

Writing task

Write the report for the club committee meeting. In your report you should:
- explain the problems the club has with membership
- explain the advantages/disadvantages and costs of each option
- suggest which you think would be best for the club.

Practice paper: Reading

This practice paper has been written to help you practise what you have learned and may not be representative of a real exam paper.

60 minutes

The total mark for this paper is 30.

INSTRUCTIONS

- Use **black** ink or ball-point pen.
- Answer **all** questions.
- Answer the questions in the spaces provided – there may be more space than you need.

Read Text A, Text B and Text C, then answer questions 1–13.

Text A

Trouble sleeping?

It's just after 8 p.m. and in small, dark rooms all around me people are lying still and silent on narrow metal beds with electrodes clamped on to their heads. It looks like something from a science fiction film or like a prison for insomniacs. In fact, I'm at the Thamesway Sleep Centre, a clinic designed to diagnose and treat sleep disorders.

A new study suggests that over 70% of us have at some point had difficulty getting to sleep and around 30% of people suffer from chronic sleep deprivation. In the short term, lack of sleep can cause stress and anxiety, whilst long-term sufferers are at risk of a weakened immune system.

As an extremely light sleeper, who suffers from lots of colds, I've checked in to the sleep clinic hoping to find some answers and cure my chronic insomnia. Staying at the clinic overnight means I can be monitored and given advice about how to adjust my sleep patterns.

I don't usually go to sleep until about 11.30 p.m., so being in my pyjamas at 8 p.m. reminds me of being at sleepovers when I was younger. I try to get into the spirit of the experiment as I am told that there is a direct link between going to bed early and being successful.

Teenagers who stay here get to 'lie in' until after 6 a.m. because young people's body rhythms mean they are not at their best until later in the morning. I will be woken at 4 a.m. – apparently being an early bird is as good for your health as an early night.

Unfortunately for my health, I last only 30 minutes before bolting for the door. Despite lying back with eye patches in place, no wave of tiredness washes over me. The electrodes grip my temples like a vice and the mattress is so thin and narrow I feel like I am trying to sleep on a concrete pavement.

Text B

Live well to sleep well

Falling asleep can seem like an impossible dream at 3 a.m. Particularly if you have followed all the popular advice, such as avoiding caffeine after 8 p.m., darkening your room, and putting lavender under your pillow. Research suggests that we need 8 hours' sleep a night to function effectively and regularly getting less than this can cause long-term harm to our heart and our joints.

Sometimes the solution lies not in your bedtime routine, but in what you do during the day. Try experimenting with these ideas for simple changes you can make to your daily routine.

Go with your natural rhythms

Try to go to sleep and get up at the same time every day as this will set your body's internal clock. Don't take a nap in the day as this will disrupt your sleep rhythms. Whilst teenagers' body clocks don't really wake until late morning, most adults would benefit from getting up early. Several studies suggest that those who don't lie in, even at weekends, are more alert and productive at work.

Get some exercise

Build some exercise into your daily routine. The more vigorously you exercise, the more powerful the sleep benefits. But even just walking for 10 minutes a day can improve the quality of your sleep.

Avoid over-thinking

Try not to spend all day worrying about your lack of sleep as this can lead to other problems. Many people who struggle to sleep put themselves under unnecessary stress by constantly looking for solutions, and modern technology makes it even easier to do this. If you find yourself surfing the net for sleep cures, distract yourself by going for a walk or listening to some relaxing music.

Eat or drink smartly

There are things you can eat that will improve the quality of your sleep. For your evening meal, choose protein foods that are rich in the amino acid 'tryptophan'. This helps boost the sleep-inducing hormone melatonin. Chicken and turkey, milk and dairy, nuts and seeds are all good choices.

Text C

The sleep secrets of successful people

Some of the most successful people claim to get by on only four hours' sleep a night. So, am I wasting my time sleeping? Mike Lawless of the Sleep Clinic thinks I might be. He says that whilst most of us get six to eight hours' sleep a night, it is possible to thrive on less than five hours.

Lawless surveyed over 100 of the country's top earners to find out their sleep secrets. While the majority followed the standard advice, sleeping at regular times, avoiding caffeine, and investing in thick curtains, a significant number did exactly the opposite. All of them survived on less than six hours' sleep a night.

Many of them recognised the virtue of daytime naps. "I nap at my desk, I nap on the train and I nap anywhere else I can snatch 10 minutes," said Sarah Mortimer, owner of a busy London hotel.

Another sleep secret came from the manager of a top football team, who believes in sleeping only when he's tired, not just when the clock says it's time to go to bed. He works for long stretches of more than 48 hours, fuelled by hot coffee, and then crashes out regardless of whether it is day or night. His lack of a sleep routine must be effective because his team are at the top of their division.

'Rising early' was one sleep secret shared by nearly all of the 100. A typical day for Frank Carter, who runs a large transport firm, starts at 4.35 a.m., when he rises without an alarm. He started these early mornings as a child and pours scorn on the idea that teenagers need a later start. "Anybody getting up later than 6 a.m. is just lazy."

Modern technology is also being used as a sleep aid by some successful people. 30% used their phones to wake them from short daytime naps, and several even used InstaSnooze, an app that claims to sooth users into a deep 4-hour sleep within 5 minutes.

1 The writer of Text A believes that:

☐ **A** most people find getting to sleep easy

☐ **B** having your sleep monitored can cure colds

☐ **C** getting up late is good for you

☐ **D** being monitored while sleeping is uncomfortable

(Total for Question 1 = 1 mark)

2 In Text A, what do the following quotations suggest about the writer's view of sleep clinics?

'like a prison for insomniacs'

....

....

'The electrodes grip my temples like a vice'

....

....

(Total for Question 2 = 2 marks)

3 What is the **main** purpose of Text A?

....

....

(Total for Question 3 = 1 mark)

4 Give **one** reason why Text B is the most suitable for someone who is struggling to get to sleep at night.

....

....

(Total for Question 4 = 1 mark)

5 In Text B, the paragraph beginning 'Falling asleep can seem like an impossible dream...' implies that:

☐ **A** drinking coffee prevents people sleeping

☐ **B** popular advice about sleep is very useful

☐ **C** following advice is the best way to sleep better

☐ **D** not all popular advice is useful

(Total for Question 5 = 1 mark)

6 In Text B, the sentence 'Build some exercise into your daily routine' is an example of:

☐ **A** a command

☐ **B** a rhetorical question

☐ **C** an exclamation

☐ **D** reported speech

(Total for Question 6 = 1 mark)

7 Explain **two** ways the writer of Text C tries to convince the reader of the benefits of having less sleep. Give an example to support each answer.

1 ....

....

....

2 ....

....

....

(Total for Question 7 = 4 marks)

8 Your friend does not believe that the amount of sleep you have has any effect on your health. Using Text A and Text B, advise your friend on the health effects of not having enough sleep.

....

....

....

....

....

....

....

....

....

(Total for Question 8 = 5 marks)

9 Give **one** quotation from Text A and **one** quotation from Text B which convey the view that young people need to wake up later in the morning.

Quotation from Text A:

....

....

....

Quotation from Text B:

....

....

....

(Total for Question 9 = 2 marks)

10   Use Text B and Text C to answer this question.

Explain how these texts have different ideas about sleep.

Give examples from each text to support your answer.

....

....

....

....

(Total for Question 10 = 5 marks)

11   You are preparing a talk on the dangerous effects modern technology has on sleep.

Which text is the **most** useful when preparing your presentation?

Give **one** reason for your choice and **one** example to support your answer.

Text ....

Reason ....

....

Example ....

....

(Total for Question 11 = 3 marks)

12   You are considering going to bed earlier to make you more successful at work.

Identify **one** piece of evidence from **each** of the three texts which shows going to sleep earlier will make you more successful at work.

Text A ....

....

Text B ....

....

Text C ....

....

(Total for Question 12 = 3 marks)

13   Which statement below is an accurate summary of points made in the texts?

☐   **A**   Texts A and B both claim that people should go to bed at 8 p.m.

☐   **B**   Texts B and C both state that people who sleep in are lazy.

☐   **C**   Texts B and C both promote different types of sleep pattern.

☐   **D**   Texts A and C both argue that lack of sleep causes health issues.

(Total for Question 13 = 1 mark)

Practice paper: Writing

This practice paper has been written to help you practise what you have learned and may not be representative of a real exam paper.

60 minutes

The total mark for this paper is 30.

INSTRUCTIONS

- Use **black** ink or ball-point pen.
- Answer **all** questions.
- Answer the questions in the spaces provided – there may be more space than you need.

Task 1

Information

A new housing estate has been built in your area. The local newspaper is asking local people to write articles about the local area to help newcomers to settle in. You decide to write one about the town centre attractions.

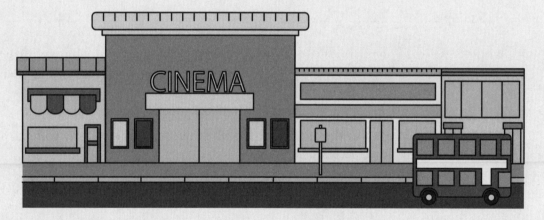

You make the following notes:

- Cinema & bowling complex, open until 11pm
- High Street with variety of shops
- Skateboard park & adventure playground
- Restaurants & cafes – including takeaways
- Estate is on bus route to town centre

Writing task

Write an article for your local newspaper about your area's town centre attractions.

In your article you should:

- describe the town's attractions
- explain who would enjoy the attractions and why
- give any advice about the town that you think would be useful.

Use sentences and write in Standard English.

(Total for Task 1 = 15 marks)

Task 2

Information

You read the following in your local newsletter.

Burstone Town Carnival needs you!

You have almost certainly been to our Carnival and remember it as a fun and exciting day out for all the family. The Carnival raises thousands of pounds for local charities every year but is only able to do this through the efforts of volunteers.

In order to make sure this year's event is as fantastic as ever we need help with the following:

*   publicity
*   running a stall – cake or produce stalls always do well but new stalls are always welcome!
*   selling tickets
*   car parking – stewards are needed
*   craft workshops

If you are enthusiastic and have spare time, we could really use your help!

Email jamie.dylan@example.com for more details.

Writing task

Write an email to Jamie offering to help in one or more areas.

In your email you should:

*   identify any areas that interest you and explain why
*   describe what qualities you have that make you suitable as a volunteer.

You may include any other information.

Remember to write in sentences and use Standard English.

(Total for Task 2 = 15 marks)

Answers

1. Your reading and writing tests

1 C

2 About 5 minutes

3 Read the question; Read the text; Annotate the text.

4

Planning Task 1	5 minutes
Writing and checking Task 1	25 minutes
Planning Task 2	5 minutes
Writing and checking Task 2	25 minutes

5 Read the task carefully.

Produce a brief plan.

2. Online tools 1

1 Answers could include:

- so you don't waste time during the test

- so that you know how to read the test clearly online.

2 **Help:** You can click this icon if you want a demonstration of how the online test buttons work.

Previous and Next: These buttons move you from question to question.

Quit: Be very careful with this icon. If you click on it and then select 'Yes', you will not be able to return to the test, even if you haven't finished!

3 **Switch colours:** This changes the colour of the text to make it easier to read.

Zoom reset: This takes the text back to the original size.

Colour reset: This takes the text back to the original colour.

Up arrow: This allows you to move around the page when you are zoomed in.

3. Online tools 2

1 You can make a plan for writing questions.

2 For example: You can make headings or titles bold.

You can underline headings.

You can right-align text to put an address on the right side of the page for a letter.

3 You can flag a question and then return to it later using the review button.

4 B

4. Reading texts

1 3

2 For example: 1 main ideas 2 purpose 3 audience

3 Cycling; heading could be underlined.

4 B

5. Skimming for details

1 Titles or headings

Numbers

2 Read the questions carefully.

3 For example: It is about spending less.

4 For example: The writer thinks the cost of living is rising but it is possible to do something about it.

5 For example: It suggests the purpose is to advise.

6. Underlining

1 Answer is given on page 6.

The first section, as it suggests hand signals are important in heavy traffic.

2 The second section, as that is about health rather than safety.

3 Relevant sections of Text B should be underlined.

7. Types of question

1 All three.

2 Evidence from the text.

3 You can paraphrase the text (put it into your own words)

4 For example: Think about what the question is asking you to do/work out what you need to include in an answer/mention the names of the texts you are writing about.

5 For example: Read all the options carefully/look at how many marks are available to see how many answers are needed.

8. Reading test skills

1 For example: Skim read the texts to find the most relevant; read the most relevant one carefully; write the answer and include the name of the text, a reason and an example from the text.

2 There is no explanation or example.

3 A

4 For example: You might want to use your own knowledge but you should only use the information in the texts.

9. Analysing texts

1 Just the paragraph starting 'When something catches their eye'.

2 7 minutes

3 C

10. Putting it into practice

1–3 Key words should be underlined in question and appropriate parts of texts underlined.

4 For example: Text D suggests that cheap fashion is a good idea as it allows you to wear 'copies of catwalk creations'. However, Text F suggests that this cheap clothing is made in 'horrific conditions'.

11. Identifying the main idea

1 For example: How to look good on a budget – how to buy nice clothes with little money

Cycle your way to health - how cycling can help you get healthy

Superfoods for family health – how to buy food that will keep your family healthy.

2 For example: The title suggests that it is about fashion that changes quickly. The first two paragraphs then show that the main idea is cheap fashion.

3 For example: The title suggests that is about how our cheap clothes are not really that cheap. Reading more of the text shows that the main idea is actually about how bad the conditions are in the places that produce the cheap clothes.

12. Texts that instruct

1 For example: The text has numbered points. This suggests that you need to read the information in a particular order.

2 Command verbs: buy, consider

Straightforward language: for example: 'any good bike will do'

3 Adult as suggests the amount of exercise necessary to be healthy – 'at least 150 minutes' – and adults are more likely to respond to this type of message.

4 For example: The main purpose is to advise people about the way in which cycling can help them get fit and instruct them how to get started.

13. Texts that inform

1 B & D

2 For example: fact – 'one of the cyclists in the incredibly successful British team'; statistic – 'sales of bikes have increased by 20%'

3 For example: Adults as they are more likely to understand ideas like the 'government's ride to work scheme'.

4 For example: The writer wants the reader to cycle more and think about cycling to work.

14. Texts that persuade

1 & 2 quotations/statistics – with arrows to these in text.

3 C

4 For example: The purpose is to persuade the reader that buying cheap fashion is a bad idea as the clothes are made in factories with no safety standards.

15. Language techniques 1

1 For example: descriptive language – 'healthy, balanced diet'; emotive language – 'debt mountain'.

2 For example: The writer has used informal language to make the writing more personal as this is more likely to make the reader follow the advice.

3 For example: an informal style – 'learn to love your oven'.

4 D

16. Language techniques 2

1 For example: rhetorical question – 'So what exactly do car drivers hold against their two-wheeled enemies?'; repetition – 'It's not'.

2 For example: hyperbole is used to express the aggression motorists feel towards cyclists on the road.

3 B & C

17. Fact and opinion

1 A = opinion; B = fact; C = expert evidence

2 makes a writer's point of view clear – opinion; can be direct or reported speech = expert evidence.

3 A

4 'At the very least…'

18. Putting it into practice

3 For example: To inform the reader about the popularity/health benefits of cycling

6 B

7 For example:

1 The writer uses repetition of 'It's not' to emphasise the bad feelings about cyclists.

2 The writer uses expert evidence like 'car drivers would be fined' to show how unfairly car drivers are treated compared with cyclists.

19. Implicit meaning 1

1 For example: 'creeping up again' – suggests it is rising slowly without people noticing; 'slash your shopping bills' – suggests it is possible to make a very big and sudden difference.

2 C

20. Implicit meaning 2

1 For example: 'dive into those tubs of scarves'

2 For example: 'by adding inexpensive accessories'

3 For example: 'stops piles of clothes being dumped into landfill sites'

21. Point of view

1 the whole text

2 opinions; language; facts; biased

3 A

4 B and C

5 Fact: 'the average UK family now spends more on ready meals, restaurant dining and takeaways than they spend on food for meal preparation'

Opinion: 'it might be time to live like your grandmother'

22. Putting it into practice

1 B

2 For example: 'less than the price of a takeaway for two' suggests that fashion is now cheap enough for everybody to afford nice clothes.

'you just need to play the game' – there is a system to buying things in sales.

5 D

9 For example: Text D – 'good news for the environment'; Text E – 'much more environmentally friendly'

23. Using more than one text

1 1 Read all the questions carefully.

3 Make it clear which text you are writing about.

4 Read all the texts in the question carefully.

2 C

3 B

4 Quotation B is not suitable because it comes from Text I and question 10 refers to Texts G and H.

24. Selecting quotations

1 A = quotation; B = paraphrase; C = both; D = quotation

2 A

3 The writer uses emotive language like 'horror stories' and 'abuse' to highlight how cheap clothing has led to poor working conditions in the past.

4 The writer uses statistics, 'as many as 600 workers', to highlight how many people work in the poor conditions.

25. Using texts 1

1 Text I

2 It is most suitable because it is about what family meal times are like, rather than how to make them better.

3 For example: 'Two younger children are eating chicken nuggets and chips'.

4 For example: Text H; Reason: because it gives practical advice in numbered points. Example: 'Fresh fruit and vegetables are the only 'superfoods' you need'.

26. Using texts 2

1 question; focus; skim; underline

2 C

3 For example: Text G – 'eating our five portions of fruit and veg a day helps'; Text H – 'Fresh fruit and vegetables are the only 'superfoods' you need'; Text I – 'using healthy fruit and vegetables'.

27. Putting it into practice

11 For example: Text A; Reason: it gives details about how many people cycle; Example: 'more people than ever are joining cycling clubs'.

12 For example: Text A = 'Cycling provides an excellent all-round workout'; Text B = 'Cycling is one of the best ways to get more active'; Text C = 'it is undoubtedly better for our health than sitting in a car'.

28. Summarising 1

1 expand on

2 options; consider; main ideas; wrong; evidence

3 C

4 They both suggest that cycling is easy, but they do not mention it is easy to do every day.

5 For example: Text B and C both stress the importance of reading The Highway Code in order to stay safe when cycling.

29. Summarising 2

1 A = 2; B = 4; D = 3

2 2 – Both texts suggest that to eat healthily on a budget it is a good idea to eat vegetarian meals. Text H says 'go vegetarian for at least one meal a week' and Text I suggests that vegetarian meals contain more 'healthy fruit and vegetables'.

30. Writing a longer answer

1 For example: secondly, also, similarly.

2 For example: for example, for instance.

3 For example: similarities: likewise, both; differences: on the other hand, by contrast.

4 For example: One difference is what the texts say about factory inspections. For instance, Text D states that factories are now inspected on a regular basis so they must be better. However, Text F suggests that the inspections are not working as inspectors are 'only taken to the best parts of the factory'.

31. Responding to a text 1

1 select; relevant; particular; purpose; advise

2 For example: adults or parents

3 For example: child safety

4 B

5 For example: Answer A is too general and Answer C is about cycling, not safety.

32. Responding to a text 2

1 C

2 A = 3; C = 2

3 For example: Secondly, you could use charity shops. Text E says you should 'buy from charity shops' and Text D suggests that this is so popular that 'charity store sales are now booming.'

33. Putting it into practice

4 Answers should give a clear explanation.

8 Answers should use a clear structure, clear evidence and appropriate connectives.

13 C

34. Using a dictionary for reading

1 Answers should give clear definitions.

2 For example: manufacture = make or produce; labour = work; adopted = taken up; sweatshop = a place with poor working conditions; cast-offs = things people do not want

35. Avoiding common mistakes

1 The student has not read the question carefully and has given the topic of the text, not the purpose.

2 For example: The answer is not fully explained.

3 Underlined key words in the question.

4 For example: 1 – The writer has used informal language, 'splashing out', which suggests eating out is a luxury. 2 – The writer uses statistics like 'the total cost is £35' to highlight how much families are wasting on takeaways.

36. Checking your work

1 5 minutes

2 For example: Check your quotations/check reasons have been given as well as examples/check the correct number of answers has been given to multiple choice questions.

3 & 4 Key words should be underlined and mistakes corrected.

37. Writing test skills

1 writing; detailed; point; believable; audience

2 For example: You should start a new paragraph for each new point or topic.

3 For example: It is important as it makes the writing more interesting.

38. Writing test questions

1 For example: Because it gives background information to the task.

2 For example: So that you can identify the audience, purpose and format.

3 Audience: probably adults as they are likely to be more interested in parking issues; they will be local people.

Purpose: to inform people about the parking issue and persuade them to take action.

Format: article – this is made clear in the task.

39. Letters, emails and reports

1 B

3 For example: It is the most formal, and you want the letter to be taken seriously.

4 For example: Title: Britown's Children's Charity. Introduction: Britown's Kids Club is the town's biggest children charity. It specialises in organising and funding once-in-a-lifetime trips for terminally ill children.

40. Articles and reviews

1 For example: 1 – Is your pavement permanently blocked? 2 – Pavement parking – coming to a street near you.

2 For example: 1 – Safety issues 2 – Retail worries

3 For example: Tram trouble or Tram triumph.

4 For example: The carpet of litter wasn't a great start to my first journey. To be fair, I hadn't waited long at the tram stop, and that was well lit and had no graffiti.

41. Speeches

2 For example: Children's health will be put at serious risk if this proposal goes ahead.

3 For example: Fact – There are no other play facilities suitable for the under-fives. Statistic – 60% of those questioned felt this was a major issue. Opinion – Young lives will be harmed by this proposal.

4 For example: I urge you to take this issue seriously. I am sure you do not want to feel responsible for a generation of children having no access to a safe and secure area in which to enjoy nature.

42. Putting it into practice

1 Key words should be underlined.

2 Table should be completed with key features.

43. Inform, explain, describe, review

1 • Signage best option: 5

• Signage – students would be motivated if work was displayed: 1

• Visitors' system – saves staff costs on reception: 3

• Signage – creates extra work as needs staff to update regularly: 2

• Visitors' system – no real advantage to students: 4

2 For example: Signage & Visitors system

3 A & E

44. Argue and persuade

1 For example: How unfit your friends are/50% of people who are obese die young/how the challenge could help/research suggests regular exercise improves life expectancy.

2 For example: I realise that you might think you have plenty of time to get fit. You may think you are young and can start exercising in a few years' time. However, it is never too early to start. Research suggests…

3 All except full stops.

45. Audience

1 Article: audience depends on who reads the newspaper; for instance, if it is a community newspaper the audience may be both adults and children Review: might have a wide audience but will depend on where it is going

to appear Report: needs to be factual and informative whoever it is intended for Letter: audience will usually be one specific person who can be addressed directly

3 For example: Many children who live locally have no back gardens, therefore the adventure playground is a valuable place for them to play outside. If the playground is removed, they may end up playing in the street, which is dangerous.

46. Formal writing

1 For example: for an official purpose, when writing to some one you don't know, when you are writing to complain.

2 Reports, letters & articles

3 Slang, text language

4 For example: Dear Mr Edwards

Hi, I am writing to you as I hope that you will think my charity deserves the grant. We are the only charity specialising in raising funds for children with rare types of cancer.

47. Informal writing

1 For example: you know your audience well, your purpose is to be friendly.

2 Dear Mr Smith

3 contractions/informal phrases/complete sentences

4 For example: Hi, I'm writing to let you know about a great challenge advertised in the paper. I think we'd all love it and get loads out of taking part in such a brilliant fitness idea.

I think we should all go for the outdoor boot camp! I bet you've also piled on the pounds since you started sitting behind a desk all day.

48. Putting it into practice

1 Answers should use an appropriately formal style and include features that are suitable for audience and purpose.

49. Planning

1 information; audience; task; bullet points; ideas

2 For example: couch potatoes; all unfit; need to get fit for our families; we will feel healthier

50. Using detail

1 C

2 All the options should be included except statistics.

3 For example: big screen – could show sporting events and film nights, wide audience could bring lots of new members.

51. Paragraphs

1 D

2 Articles & letters

3 paragraph; topic; introduces; sentencesl develop; topic

4 For example: Prefer relaxing hols now grown up/Never been on cruise/Love spas.

52. Point–Evidence–Explain

1 point; evidence; details; sentence; detail; explain

2 Statistics/examples from experience.

3 P.E.E. should be labelled.

4 For example: Another idea is to show films and sports on a big screen every week, which could appeal to a lot of different people. For example, we could show a romantic comedy one week and a horror movie the next. This would make sure that the club was offering something for everyone.

53. Linking ideas

1 Adding an idea: in addition, furthermore, additionally

Explaining: consequently, therefore

Introducing evidence: for example

Comparing and contrasting: likewise, in the same way, in contrast, however similarly

Ordering points: firstly, secondly, next, finally, in conclusion

2 **Firstly**, I would like to state that I strongly disagree with Estrick Council's proposals. **Furthermore**, I think many local residents feel the same way.

Sharpness Woods is a well-known and well-loved local beauty spot. **For example**, many families go for the day, taking a picnic and using the adventure playground. The playground provides a safe area for children to play in the fresh area and it is the only outdoor play area for several miles. Removing it would, **therefore**, be a serious issue for local families.

3 For example: Secondly, the woods provide a natural habitat for many species of bird. For instance, the reed warbler, which is only found in two other places in the UK. Similarly, the dormouse, extinct in many other areas, is found in the woods. Consequently, keeping the woods in their current state is very important.

54. Putting it into practice

1&2 Answers should include a detailed plan and two paragraphs using an appropriate style and a clear P.E.E. structure using adverbials to link points.

55. Vocabulary

1 For example: stop – avoid/resist/prevent; sitting – reclining/slouching; getting – becoming

2 For example: issue – problem/subject; think – consider/dwell on; bad – serious/awful; nice – terrific/great/helpful/positive; take – spend/steal

3 For example: We all need to accept that we have **a problem** with our weight. Please **spend** some time **considering how** we can **prevent** ourselves from **slouching** for hours in front of the TV. Not only is this a really **harmful** thing for our weight, but it is also **preventing** us **socialising** with our friends. Taking up a fitness challenge would help us to lose weight, and I am sure you will agree that it would be **terrific** to spend some time together.

56. Language techniques 1

1 1 = rhetorical question; 2 = repetition; 3 = direct address; 4 = lists; 5 = direct address; 6 = lists

2 For example: The park is used extensively by local people. The many benefits to them include: it is a safe area for children to play, it is a pleasant place to exercise, it has an interesting nature trail and it is a haven for wildlife. Do you really want to be responsible for taking all these away?

57. Language techniques 2

1 (a) = personification; (b) = metaphor; (c) = alliteration; (d) = simile; (f) = personification

2 For example: Mountains of doughnuts met my eye as I looked around me in wonder. The smell of fried onions rushed towards me from a hot dog stall. I felt like a child in a sweet shop as I walked from one food stall to another. All seemed to be stacked with so many delicious delicacies waiting to be savoured.

58. Putting it into practice

Answers should include vocabulary for effect and a suitable range of language techniques for impact.

59. Sentences

1 (a) will travel
 (b) will join
 (c) walk
 (d) enjoyed
 (e) will help
 (f) walk
 (g) ran/went

2 (a) I
 (b) Simon
 (c) I
 (d) Ben
 (e) The pedestrian zone
 (f) Local residents
 (g) The trams/I

3 For example:
 (a) but
 (b) because
 (c) bus
 (d) he will need more training

4 For example: I walk to the gym every day, although I hate it when it is raining. Ben enjoyed the funfair therefore, he will go again tomorrow.

Local residents walk in the woods, however not after dark.

5 For example: We could hire a big screen on a regular basis and show sporting events. It would also be good to show films as this would bring in a wider audience who might want to become members. However, I think we should let our current members vote on this idea as the hire of the screen might be expensive.

60. Sentence variety

1 For example: Near my house, there is a homeless shelter where I volunteer./Running a market stall gave me valuable organisational skills./Beautiful parks like those we have locally should be kept clear of litter./Importantly, I have experience of managing people.

2 For example: I would be very interested in helping out with the 'Help a Neighbour' scheme. Elderly people are very vulnerable if they have no family so I believe it is a valuable cause. Running errands for them could easily be fitted in around my job. Alternatively, I could spend one day helping out every other weekend.

61. Writing about the present and future

1 (a) hope/consider; (b) exercise; (c) encourage;
(d) loves/visits; (e) play/walk; (f) park/lacks

2 For example: (a) play; (b) is/meet; (c) aims
(d) win/love; (e) park/walk

3 (a) Ben is going to run in the park every day during the Fitness Challenge.

(b) I am going to volunteer at the animal shelter every day in the summer.

(c) We are going to raise money for the hospital scanner appeal by swimming a mile.

4 For example: We will have to work hard at the challenge./Ben will spend more if he joins a gym./I will send a letter about the state of the tram next time it is dirty.

62. Writing about the past

1 (a) applied; (b) complained; (c) filled; (d) worked;
(e) parked; (f) wasted

2 (b) cried; (c) hurried; (d) carried

3 (a) = did; (b) were; (c) had; (d) saw; (e) got; (f) ate;
(g) made

63. Putting it into practice

Answers should include a variety of sentence styles and openings. Sentences should include detail, linking words and be in the correct tense throughout.

64. Full stops and capital letters

1 A capital letter

2 For example: names of places, the month in a date

3 With an exclamation mark.

4 (a) The charity fashion show starts at 8pm. Mrs Jones and her daughter Janet will be providing the refreshments.

(b) I think everybody should spend time exercising in the fresh air. My friend pays far too much each month to go to a gym.

(c) I had my wedding at the Broxtown Social Club. A jazz band plays there every Saturday night.

5 (a) Why should dog owners be forced to go miles into the countryside to exercise their pets?

(b) I was so scared on the rollercoaster I had to shut my eyes!

(c) I am not happy with the way you have handled my complaint about the tram.

65. Commas

1 ✓ Our charity is dedicated to helping carers and we can offer financial support, a day centre with a variety of activities and transport to and from hospital appointments.

✓ Anybody can get fit on this challenge; it doesn't matter whether you are thin, tall, fat, short, young, or old.

✓ The tram seats, which I would have liked to test for comfort, had litter on them.

✓ Our profits, which last year were over £500, are all dedicated to good causes.

2 (a) If they are planned carefully, pedestrian zones can help with parking problems.

(c) As it is a popular local beauty spot, efforts should be made to keep the area free of housing.

3 For example: I have experience of serving the public, managing a team of people and organising publicity for large events. As I have experience of publicity, I think I would be ideal as a volunteer for the Library reading group. Estrick Council, where I worked for over five years, would be able to give me a reference.

66. Apostrophes and inverted commas

1 ✓ Visitors to the funfair on a Saturday will be able to watch an open air showing of 'Punch and Judy'.

✓ "Roll up, roll up!" is the familiar cry from the funfair stalls.

✓ I was described by my last employer as 'the safest pair of hands' he had ever come across.

2 (a) My friend's gym charges over £50 a month.

(b) The café at the funfair has a children's menu.

(c) We are very proud of our charity's work.

(d) Friends of the Park is a really valuable community group.

(e) My school's sports facilities are the best in the city.

3 (a) don't; (b) I've; (c) I'm; (d) can't; (e) I've/I'll

67. Spelling tips

1 (a) believe
(b) science
(c) receive
(d) deceive
(e) receipt
(f) friend

2 (a) address
(b) different
(c) tomorrow
(d) disappoint
(e) possible
(f) disappear
(g) embarrass
(h) recommend

3 (a) safely
(c) When/which
(d) extremely/whole
(e) half/Wednesday/autumn
(f) definitely/when

68. Common spelling errors 1

1. (a) to/they're
(b) to/two
(c) wear/our
(d) you're/off/too
(e) are/of
(f) were/our
(g) they're
(h) there/your/to

2 (a) are/their
(b) were/were/we're/our/our
(c) we're/to/our
(d) wear
(e) there/to
(f) our/too

69. Common spelling errors 2

1 **(b)** could have

  (c) brought

  (d) know

  (e) write

  (f) should have; brought

2 **(a)** brought/right

  (b) would have

  (c) know

  (d) have

  (e) have/right

  (f) would have/right

  (g) no/should have

  (h) right

  (i) bought

70. Common spelling errors 3

explanation

although

because

decide

argument

happened

beautiful

interrupt

business

meanwhile

separate

unfortunately

queue

remember

persuade

straight

preparation

nervous

autumn

actually

71. Plurals

1 **(a)** tests

  (b) churches

  (c) buses

  (d) lives

  (e) glasses

  (f) boxes

  (g) plans

  (h) ourselves

2 **(b)** families/babies

  (c) cities

  (d) libraries

  (e) sundays

  (f) parties/weekdays

3 **(a)** children

  (b) people

  (c) men

  (d) women/men

  (e) feet

72. Checking your work

1 A fitness challenge is just what we need to get rid of <u>our</u> winter flab. We all <u>know</u> that we shouldn't <u>have</u> had all those crisps and beers while slumped in front <u>of</u> the TV!

Challenging <u>ourselves</u> to a series of boot camp sessions in the open air <u>would</u> be a really brilliant idea. Instead of watching yet another box set we <u>could experience</u> the great outdoors, get fit and lose weight. Fitness4u have fully <u>qualified</u> personal trainers who will look after us every step <u>of</u> the way. You need not be <u>nervous</u> about <u>injuries</u> as they <u>guarantee</u> to measure <u>our</u> fitness throughout the programme.

73. Putting it into practice

Answers should have correct spelling and punctuation. Time should have been spent checking the work and correcting any errors.

74. Putting it into practice (example answer)

Make sure you have made the improvements suggested on page 74.

75. Putting it into practice (example answer)

Make sure you have made the improvements suggested on page 75.

97. Practice paper: Reading

1 D

2 The clinics are so unpleasant that they cannot help you sleep better.

  The electrodes are very uncomfortable.

3 To persuade the reader that sleep clinics don't help people sleep better.

4 It gives advice about how to get a good night's sleep.

5 D

6 A

7 The writer argues that you don't need a lot of sleep to have a successful career. She says that 'some of the most successful people claim to get by on only four hours' sleep a night'.

  She supports her argument with an expert opinion from Mark Lawless of the Sleep Clinic.

8 Not having enough sleep is bad for your health. In the short term, it can make you stressed, and in the long term it can weaken your immune system (Text A). Another risk is damage to your heart and joints (Text B).

9 Text A: 'young people's body rhythms mean they are not at their best until later in the morning.'

  Text B: 'Whilst teenagers' body clocks don't really wake until late morning, most adults would benefit from getting up early.'

10 Text B argues that getting enough sleep is important, and that 'we need 8 hours' sleep a night to function effectively'. It recommends avoiding naps in the day, because they can 'disrupt your sleep rhythms'. In contrast, Text C argues that less sleep is be better for you. It states that that over a hundred of the highest earning people in the country sleep less than six hours a night. In addition, it quotes a business woman who takes daytime naps whenever she can.

11 Text: B

Reason: Because it talks about how technology can stop you sleeping properly.

Example: 'Many people who struggle to sleep put themselves under unnecessary stress by constantly looking for solutions, and modern technology makes it even easier to do this.'

12 Text A: 'there is a direct link between going to bed early and being successful'

Text B: People who get up early are 'more alert and productive at work'.

Text C: In the survey, nearly all the top 100 earners in the country said that they got up early.

13 C

100. Practice paper: Writing

Task 1 For example:

The town centre has something for everyone, and is just a short bus ride from the estate. High Street has a wide variety of shops, selling everything from the latest fashions to cutting edge technology and everyday bargains.

If you fancy some entertainment, head to the cinema and bowling complex. The cinema has five screens and shows many different films, from family favourites to exciting thrillers. Look out for special deals on Mondays!

The bowling is good fun too, and is very popular with families and young people. Best of all, the complex is open until 11pm every night.

Children and young people will also love the park, with its adventure playground and skateboard park. It's a safe and friendly place for them to meet up with their friends.

All that shopping, bowling and skating will work up an appetite! Luckily, the town centre has lots of fantastic cafes and restaurants to choose from. Try Emma's café for delicious cakes, or Bistro Bouffant for a high-class meal. If you want food on the move, there are also plenty of takeaways.

Task 2 For example:

To: jamiedylan@example.com

Burston Town Carnival volunteers

Dear Jamie,

I would like to offer to volunteer at the Burston Town Carnival. I've enjoyed going to the carnival since I was a child, and would like to help support it.

I'm particularly interested in running a jewellery making workshop. I have always loved making things, and now run a successful business selling my jewellery designs online. In addition, I have managed a local art and craft club for two years, so I'm good at explaining things to people. Finally, I could get supplies at a good price from my cousin, who owns an art and craft shop in Estrick.

I look forward to hearing from you.

Best wishes,

Nisha Sharma

Published by Pearson Education Limited, 80 Strand, London, WC2R 0RL.

www.pearsonschoolsandfecolleges.co.uk

Copies of official specifications for all Edexcel qualifications may be found on the website: www.edexcel.com

Text © Pearson Education Limited 2017
Edited, typeset and produced by Elektra Media Ltd
Original illustrations © Pearson Education Limited 2017
Illustrated by Elektra Media Ltd
Cover illustration by Miriam Sturdee

The right of Julie Hughes to be identified as author of this work has been asserted by her in accordance with the Copyright, Designs and Patents Act 1988.

First published 2017

20 19 18 17
10 9 8 7 6 5 4 3 2 1

British Library Cataloguing in Publication Data
A catalogue record for this book is available from the British Library

ISBN 978 1 292 14579 2

Printed in Slovakia by Neografia